Walks in the Cairngorms

ERNEST CROSS

Luath Press Limited

EDINBURGH

www.luath.co.uk

First Edition 1984
Reprinted 1984
Revised Edition 1985
Reprinted 1986
Reprinted 1987
Revised Edition 1988
New Edition 1990
Reprinted 1991
Revised Edition 1992
Revised Edition 1993
New Edition 1994
Revised Edition 1995
Revised Edition 1996
Revised Edition 1997
Reprinted 1997
Reprinted 1998
Revised Edition 2000

This book is made from low-chlorine pulps produced in a
low-energy, low-emission manner from renewable forests
and from recycled materials, the latter comprising at
least 50% of the pulps used.

Printed and bound by
Gwasg Dinefwr Press Ltd., Llandybie

Typeset in 10 point Sabon by
Senga Fairgrieve, Edinburgh, 0131 658 1763

In memory of Patricia and Dennis Rosenfield,
whose hospitality was a byword in these byways.
For Phil and Ben, good companions on so many
happy Cairngorm days. And for Pat, who lets me
off the leash each year.

Map Notes

The sketch maps indicate the direction and duration of the walks, but they should be used only for walk planning. THEY ARE NOT A SUBSTITUTE FOR A PROPER MAP. The Visitors' Guide to Rothiemurchus will do for walks 1 & 5 in good weather, but, overall, a good map is essential.

Three OS maps cover the area:

Cairngorm Tourist Map, 1 inch : 1 mile
Grantown and Cairngorm, 1 : 50,000
Aviemore and the Cairngorms, 1 : 25,000

Harvey's walkers maps cover the main mountain area.
Choice will depend on personal preference.
National Grid references are used in walk descriptions.

NOTE: most large scale maps continue to show Jean's Hut in Coire an Lochain (NH981034) and Sinclair Hut in the Lairig Ghru (NH959036). NOTE THAT THESE REFUGES WERE DISMANTLED AND REMOVED SOME YEARS AGO.

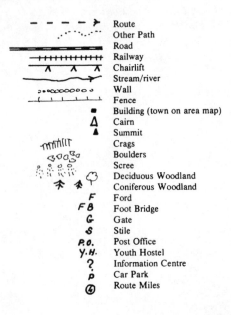

Symbol	Meaning
– – – – ➤	Route
·· ··· ··	Other Path
▬▬▬▬▬	Road
+++++++++++	Railway
⋏ ⋏ ⋏	Chairlift
～～～➤	Stream/river
∘∘∞∞∘∘∘∘∘	Wall
─┴─┴─┴─	Fence
■	Building (town on area map)
∆	Cairn
▲	Summit
ᴍᴍᴍ	Crags
♋ᴏ♋	Boulders
∘:∘∘∘	Scree
♧	Deciduous Woodland
♣ ♣	Coniferous Woodland
F	Ford
F B	Foot Bridge
G	Gate
S	Stile
P.O.	Post Office
Y.H.	Youth Hostel
?	Information Centre
P	Car Park
④	Route Miles

Acknowledgements

Background information has been slowly absorbed over more years than I care to remember, so it is difficult to be specific about any source. however, recognition must be given to that excellent HMSO publication 'Glenmore Forest Park – Cairngorms', which provides so much valuable information for the interested visitor. Forest Enterprise staff have always been helpful.

I must record my indebtedness to Ben Gardner, who bullied me into this book, and provided the basic route notes for walks 1, 3 and 6.

Thanks are due to the Chief Constable of Northern Constabulary for helpful comments on safety in the hills.

Last, but not least, I must mention Hamish McGregor, of Aviemore, for the historical information gleaned from our discussions, and for guiding me to a better understanding of Highland philosophy.

A message from the Publishers

Our authors welcome feedback from their readers, so do please let us have your comments and suggestions. The feedback we have received indicates that the Walk with Luath Guides are valued by their readers and that their usefulness is enhanced by the inclusion of advertisements for local businesses whose support Luath Press greatly appreciates. We, in turn, encourage our readers to make use of their products and services. Mention Luath Press when you do. The author's editorial independence is unaffected by the inclusion of these advertisements.

Whilst we make every effort to ensure that information in our books is correct, we can accept no responsibility for any accident, loss or inconvenience arising.

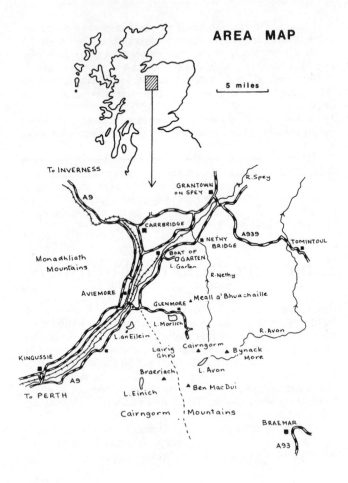

AREA MAP

5 miles

To INVERNESS

R. Spey

GRANTOWN
ON SPEY

A9

CARRBRIDGE

NETHY
BRIDGE

A939

TOMINTOUL

Monadhliath
Mountains

BOAT OF
GARTEN

L. Garten

R. Nethy

AVIEMORE

GLENMORE ▲ Meall a' Bhuachaille

L. Morlich

R. Avon

L. an Eilein

Cairngorm

Lairig
Ghru

▲ Bynack
More

KINGUSSIE

L. Avon

Braeriach

A9

▲ Ben MacDui

To PERTH

L. Einich

Cairngorm Mountains

BRAEMAR

A93

Contents

Map Notes 4
Acknowledgements 5
Message from Publisher 5
Preface 9
Foreground 11

PART ONE: FIVE FOREST WALKS 14

Rothiemurchus 14

   WALK 1   Loch an Eilein 20

   WALK 2   Two Eags 26

   WALK 3   A Day for Birdwatching ... 30

   WALK 4   Loch Morlich 34

   WALK 5   The Lairig Ghru 42

   Wayfaring 48

PART TWO: SEVEN HILL WALKS 51

Background 51

   WALK 6   The Shepherd of Glenmore ... 56

   WALK 7   Ben MacDui 64

WALK 8   Cairngorm North Ridge   70

WALK 9   Cairngorm Corries   78

WALK 10   The Bynacks   82

WALK 11   Craigellachie Nature Reserve   88

WALK 12   Eagle's Corrie   94

Safety in the Hills   99

Natural History Notes   101

Further Reading   107

Useful Information   109

Gaelic Glossary   113

Preface

THE CAIRNGORMS AREA, as a whole, is being increasingly affected by the kind of recreational and economic pressures that have created so many problems in the National Parks of England and Wales – and we are all part of that problem. A Government convened Working Party, chaired by Magnus Magnusson KBE, studied the problems and suggested various remedies. The proposals were broadly accepted, and a Cairngorms Partnership board was established in 1994 with the job of overseeing the future development of the area.

From the visitor's point of view, the main effects are as follows:

– Priority is being given to the regeneration of the existing areas of Caledonian forest, and two new forests have been designated: Strathspey and Mar.

– Where expedient, access may be controlled (this covers all land: mountain, moor and woodland).

The practical effects are beginning to be seen in and around the Queen's Forest, and in the other Forest Enterprise woodlands in the area. Rather than adopt a piecemeal approach to the problem which could, for the time being, have left attractive stands of mature trees here and there, Forest Enterprise are engaged in a rigorous programme of wholesale clearance of all non-native trees and shrubs. It is a form of arboreal ethnic cleansing, which means an end to the serried ranks of Sitka spruce, Douglas fir, Lodgepole pine and larch, etc., and has created a tremendous mess in the affected woodlands.

When our grand-children are very old there will be a new woodland of native trees throughout Strathspey. In the meantime we must put up with the devastated clearings, and take comfort in the knowledge that it is all for the common good, and that time and nature are great healers. The clearance areas should become quite attractive scrubland fairly soon.

Parking restrictions apart, there has been little impact on outdoor pursuits so far, and walk descriptions acknowledge the changes where appropriate.

The future is uncertain, and current proposals are for either a funicular or gondola-car lift to replace the chairlift on Cairngorm by 1999. To satisfy the requirements of Scottish Natural Heritage, and other conservation bodies, the new installation will be a closed system that will eliminate the easy access to Cairngorm and the plateau, other than for skiers. The golden age may be coming to an end.

Ernest Cross

Foreground

IT IS SOMETHING OF A paradox that new visitors to the Cairngorms area are often stuck for somewhere to start on a walking holiday. Everything is on a very grand scale here, the maps are notable for their lack of marked paths, and it is all rather different from the Lake District, Snowdonia, and other hill country in Britain. Alfred Wainwright came for his holidays, but he just drew the hills, so there is little in the way of published guides for walkers.

The Cairngorms are noted for their remoteness, and this poses a major problem for hill walkers. There seems to be little alternative to a long walk in and out, and this was one of the reasons for the existence and continuing presence of the low-level refuges or bothies. There are only two through routes north-south: the Lairig Ghru in the west and Lairig an Laoigh in the east. These are rough, high-level walking tracks, although some hardy (or foolhardy) cyclists do traverse them sometimes.

There is no simple answer to the overall problem, and a visit to the more remote parts of the region can only be accomplished at the cost of a very long and arduous day, or by a night out in the hills. The latter is a very dubious alternative in this region of notoriously harsh and freak weather conditions.

It is no wonder, then, that access to the mountains tends to be dominated by the easy ascent of Cairngorm, using the chairlift at the end of the road through Glenmore. In summer, large numbers of visitors, casual and otherwise, pay the fare and ride up to the Ptarmigan station. From there, they troop dutifully up the fenced path to the summit of Cairngorm and, like the Grand Old Duke of York's 10,000 men, they then troop down again. This is not a bad thing in itself, and there is a splendid view from the top, but the range offers considerably more than this. The chairlift also the major means of access for the majority of more serious walkers, most of whom seem intent on no more than an ascent of Ben MacDui. The result of the concentrated summer and winter activity is very evident, and the west face of the mountain has been severely eroded.

It has all happened before, elsewhere, and there was once a 'Golden Age' in the English Lake District when one had to search for the route over Rossett Gill - now it is like a road. There is still time to enjoy a Golden age in the Cairngorms, but not for much longer: the area grows more popular year by year, and Scottish Natural Heritage in concert with the Chairlift Company and some other bodies are planning to restrict access.

There are other things to see and do than the ascent of Ben MacDui (although that is a fine excursion), and away from Cairngorm itself there are relatively insignificant hills which would be regarded as classics in the south. In the surrounding foothills there is some hauntingly beautiful countryside which tends to be ignored by people intent on getting above the 3,000 foot contour, and it seems to have been forgotten that best views of mountains are usually to be had from somewhere below their summits.

These walks are an attempt to address some of the problems, but they represent only a tiny fraction of the possibilities for a week's walking holiday in the Cairngorms from a base in Aviemore, or somewhere nearby. They contain the distilled experience of very many visits to the area, and they should be within the

capabilities of most people who are used to hill walking in Britain. Whilst they are definitely not for 'tigers', it must be recognised that Scottish miles tend to be long, and a reasonable degree of physical fitness is assumed. If you have just vacated an office chair, then run-in gently on some forest walks before taking to the tops.

No other assumptions have been made, but advice on mountain safety is given in a special chapter, and this must not be ignored.

Rothiemurchus

THE PARISH OF ROTHIEMURCHUS – the Plain of the Great Pines – covers a large area and encompasses a wide variety of countryside. The boundary runs along the Spey, from Aviemore to just beyond Loch an Eilein, and then turns to take in Glen Einich and the Sgorans, part of Braeriach and the Lairig Ghru, and the woodland towards Loch Morlich. It continues northwards to Loch Pityoulish.

To the ordinary visitor this will appear to be a wild, rugged, and (in some places) barren land, and the fact that much of it is farmed may seem a ludicrous idea. But farmed it is, and the range of produce is wide. Animal husbandry provides cattle, sheep, deer and trout, arable farming is carried on in the riverside haughs, and timber is cropped in the forest. The land is all

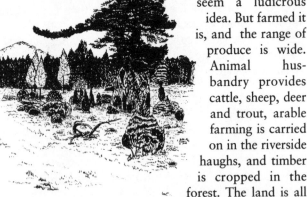

Rothiemurchus

privately owned, mainly by the Grants, who work in harmony with Scottish Natural Heritage, and the general public have been given very generous access. Much of the country is included in the National Nature Reserve.

There is a very special feel about this place, and one can enjoy a blissful solitude without feeling in any way alone. The red tracks of granite sand and pine needles wind between honeyed tussocks of russet heather. Junipers form prickly pillars in the grassy flats, their blue-bloomed berries redolent of resin and gin. Wood ants build their hills in a frenzy of activity that goes on for ever, and the boulders lie everywhere, clothed with club moss and multi-coloured lichen. Through the pine trees, green-black in the bright sunshine, Carn Eilrig dominates the landscape out of all proportion to its modest height. Aloof and alone, it guards the entrances to Glen Einich and the Lairig Ghru.

Along these tracks one is walking on history, and the forest is crossed by the Rhathad nam Mearlach – the Thieves Road – which was used by the caterans of Lochaber on their forays into the fat cattle lands of Banff and Moray. Their route through Rothiemurchus was from the Feshie, by Loch an Eilein to Loch Morlich, then through Ryvoan and across the Nethy to Tomintoul.

The MacGregors, from far away Balquhidder, who were also noted drovers and caterans, were said to have had a long association with the Rothiemurchus Grants. Seton Gordon records that the legendary Rob Roy MacGregor was said to have supported the Laird of Rothiemurchus during a bitter dispute with the Clan MacIntosh, when the MacIntoshes were threatening to burn the Doune. As a direct result of Rob Roy's intervention, the MacIntoshes were bested and the threat removed. Following this incident, two MacGregors were left behind to get help if needed, and one was given the tenancy of Aultdruie.

There are many versions of this story, but it is true

that the little farm was occupied by the MacGregors until 1890, when Hamish MacGregor, the last farmer, died. It was probably a desirable holding then, but the ruined buildings in the river flats are now a mute reminder of the hard life in centuries past.

The estate is certainly ancient, and at the time of the Norman alliance with the old Scots, it is said to have belonged to the Norman family of Comyns. They fell out of favour, and in the 14th c. Alexander Stewart, a bastard son of Robert II, acquired the estate. It then passed to the Shaws, and having been forfeited to the Crown – Scottish history is complicated – the right to the estate was purchased by the Grants, and about 1600 it was settled on Patrick, second son of the Clan's chief. It has remained in Grant hands since then, and the present laird is the thirteenth in direct succession.

Forest and Rothiemurchus are practically synonymous, and the area is always associated with woodland. But 'forest' is used here in the old sense to mean deer forest, which includes large tracts of open moor and hills. There is, of course, a great deal of wooded country, which is not Forestry Commission land, and it shows. Indeed, some of the finest remnants of the old birch and pine woodlands are found here, and are naturally regenerating, despite constant grazing by deer. As might be expected, this is a very good area for studying woodland creatures. Wildlife is abundant, and naturalists could spend a happy holiday entirely within the forest boundary.

The vast majority of people see little of the wildlife of the hills and woodlands, and there are many who conclude that this life is virtually extinct. This is not so, and one's every step is carefully observed. The fault lies in the approach, and most walkers telegraph their coming for many miles ahead.

There is a major problem concerning dress. It is popularly supposed that a red or orange anorak renders rescue more certain if one is injured or lost on the hills. This may be true, but brightly coloured clothing is easily seen by the wild things, and they go to ground or depart. The muted hues and soft shades of the traditional tweeds and hunting tartans are not a sign of natural restraint – witness the splendour of the dress plaids – nor do they signify suicidal tendencies on the part of the deer stalkers and other working hillmen. They were a practical response to the requirement for unobtrusive dress by a people whose very livelihood was closely tied to a successful hunt or pillage. The principle remains, and beige, brown and 'cowpat' green are all good colours for the country. Tweeds are in vogue again, and the ubiquitous 'Barbour' is a boon. Untreated quiet cottons, like Grenfell cloth, are worn by many serious naturalists.

Other factors are noise and vibration. To see wildlife during a walk it is necessary to tread lightly, walk softly, and refrain from chatter. Small groups are preferable to large parties, and it is an advantage to be walking into the wind. All these factors add up to one thing: minimal disturbance to the natural inhabitants of the countryside. Remember that it is their world as well as ours, and they live there whilst we are merely visitors. It is really just a form of courtesy; try it, and prepare to be surprised by the difference it will make.

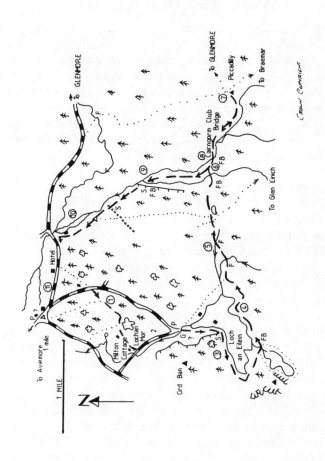

Walk 1: Loch an Eilein

THIS WALK IS, PERHAPS, the perfect introduction to Rothiemurchus, and it is a good alternative to the hills if the clouds are down, or if it is too hot to be away from shade. It traverses the 'Thieves Road' as far as Piccadilly, and the return is along the start of the Lairig Ghru track. The distance is about twelve miles, and the duration will be about five hours.

Across the way, and a little to the E of the car park by the Ranger Centre at Inverdruie (NH901110), a minor road goes roughly SE to Blackpark and Tullochgrue. Follow this road for about half a mile to where it crosses a track just before the fork by Blackpark. Turn right onto the track and carry on to the SW. Lochan Mor, about half a mile on, has plenty of wildlife, for this area is the haunt of roe deer and red squirrels, and foxes are also numerous.

The track continues past the N end of the lochan until it comes to a road that follows the course of the Milton Burn, with Ord Ban providing an impressive backdrop. In the early morning and in the evening deer come to drink here, and they are not particularly timid. Turn left and follow the road to the head of Loch an Eilein. To the right, just past the car park, there is a visitor centre with toilets. The exhibition here is of local natural history, and it should not be missed. It is of interest for its own sake, and will add greatly to the enjoyment of the walk.

Go on through the pinewoods around the W side of

the loch. The photogenic ruin on the islet is the remains of a 14/15th century stronghold, reputedly the lair of Alexander Stewart, the legendary Wolf of Badenoch – a local warlord and notorious bandit.

Birdwatchers will have a field-day, and should look for rarer species,

Wolf's Lair – Loch an Eilein

which include crested tits, crossbills and tree creepers. Ospreys also fish here from time to time, which is not really surprising, because this was their last recorded habitat in 1899, before their return to Strathspey in the 1950s. The loch is noted for its pike.

At the S end of the loch, across a footbridge, a track goes off to the right, along the E side of Loch Gamhna and on to Feshiebridge. This track can be followed to extend the walk, but the route will have to be re-traced to Loch an Eilein. The pine trees at this end of the loch are very old, and many of them would have been young saplings at the time of Bonnie Prince Charlie's rising in 1745. The prominent hill in the background is the Cats Cradle, which is known to be a breeding ground for wild cats.

Continue round the loch to a signposted track heading E, and follow it for about two miles to the river. This is the Rathad nam Mearlach – the Thieves Road - used by the freebooters of old when raiding for cattle in the east. The track passes by the confluence of two rivers: the Druie, which runs down from the Lairig Ghru, and Am Beanaidh, which flows out of Loch Einich. Crossing the river at this ford must have been an exciting experience prior to 1912, when it was bridged by the Cairngorm

Club. A plaque on the bridge commemorates the event, and another one provides an interesting list of destinations with times and distances from this spot. This is a very good place for picnics and a bathe, but be warned that the water is mainly melt water, and is usually ice-cold.

Substantial though it may seem, the bridge has obviously been severely battered by the elements over the years, and flood waters seem to have inflicted substantial damage – just a reminder that it can be unpleasant here at times. Cross the bridge and follow the Lairig Ghru track to a cross roads in the forest, where there is a large cairn and, usually, a sign post to Braemar. The local name for the junction is Piccadilly, and it is the turning point for this walk.

Another track goes off to the left, opposite the cairn. Although not part of this walk, it could be rewarding to follow this track for a little way. Obviously little used, it passes through a section of ancient woodland that is of unsurpassed beauty, and the peace and quiet here on a warm spring day will be long remembered. Normally, the only sounds here are the rustle of the breeze in the trees, the zizz of insects, and the chattering, twittering and singing of many different kinds of bird. Crashing and fluttering in the undergrowth could be capercaillies, and in flight they look like rather large black or brown turkeys. This is also wild cat country, but they will be neither seen nor heard.

Capercaillie

This magnificent bit of old woodland is part of the old Caledonian forest, and the vegetation is very lush. If you

pause for a rest at any time do be careful where you sit: wood ants are not respecters of persons, and they are numerous and always extremely agressive.

The track is obviously an old extension of the Lairig route. At one time it carried on to the river that flows out of Loch Morlich, and a long-gone pine log bridge carried the track over to the Glenmore road, and on to Coylumbridge. The old bridge abutments can still be seen close to a picnic lay-by on the Glenmore road. A branch of the track, by the river, used to lead to the 'Medicine Well', a somewhat smelly chalybeate spring of noted curative properties. In centuries past people came from as far afield as Braemar to drink the water. This part of the track is now closed off by a deer fence and cannot be explored.

Go back now to the footbridge and cross the river, and then take the track to the right, heading roughly N. The way, through juniper scrub and pinewoods, is along a sandy path that stays close to the water, and the river can be heard raging away to the right. A very large cairn on the left marks the junction with the track from Glen

Chalamain Gap

Einich. A little further on, the picturesque log cabin of Lairig Ghru Cottage heralds the conclusion of the walk, and the ski road is reached at its junction with the Nethy Bridge road. Turn left, and walk along the grassy verge for about half a mile, back to the car park.

WALK 2
TWO EAGS

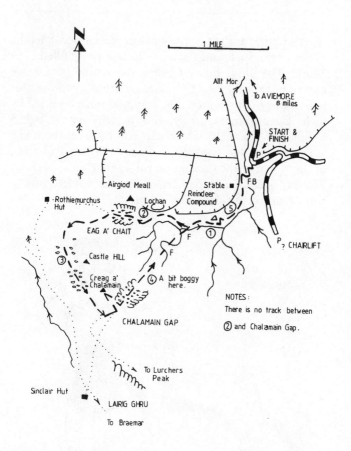

N

1 MILE

Allt Mor

To AVIEMORE
8 miles

START &
FINISH

P

FB

Stable

Reindeer
Compound

Airgiod Meall

Lochan

Rothiemurchus
Hut

②

EAG A' CHAIT

⑤

①

③

Castle HILL

F

Creag a'
Chalamain

F

④ A bit boggy
here.

CHALAMAIN GAP

P ? CHAIRLIFT

NOTES:
There is no track between
② and Chalamain Gap.

To Lurchers
Peak

Sinclair Hut

LAIRIG GHRU

To Braemar

Walk 2: Two Eags

DURING THE LAST ICE AGE a gigantic glacier occupied the valley of the Spey, and a satellite tongue of ice filled Glen More. The slow but relentless movement of the ice carved out the Ryvoan pass, and interfered with the normal drainage of the area. The resultant huge lake, fed by melt water from higher ground, overflowed through a number of channels, which can still be seen about the 2,250 ft. contour. Eagle's Corrie and the Eag a'Gharbh, at the N end of the Cairngorm ridge, are typical of these. The Eag a Chait and the Chalamain Gap resulted from a similar process in the Lairig Ghru.

BEWARE REINDEER!

Geological interest apart, the Eags provide relatively easy access to some spectacular scenery, and this walk goes through the well known Chalamain Gap, and the almost unknown, but quite interesting, Eag a'Chait. The distance is about six miles, and the duration three or four hours.

Start from the car park by the big hairpin on the ski road (NH985074). Across the road, by a 'Beware Reindeer' sign, the path goes steeply downhill to a bridge over the Allt Mor. This bridge is only the latest of many, and some remains of its predecessors can be seen downstream. When the thaw starts there are no half measures, and the force of the water is evident from the erosion in this gully. There used to be a path around the foot of the escarpment, but it was swept away by a great wash-out in 1960, and there is no alternative now to the path that climbs steeply up the banking on the other side of the stream.

The fenced compound on the right is for reindeer, and they congregate by the path every day to await the arrival of the herd's owner, and the accompanying party of sightseers. Excursions come here every day from Reindeer House in Glenmore.

Follow the peaty track along the edge of the escarpment, and down to the stream at the cairn. Stay by the stream and head uphill through the small notch of Eag a'Chait. Contour round the side of Castle Hill and Creag a' Chalamain, following the deer tracks, and trying to maintain height. After about a mile the Chalamain track will be seen coming in from the gap to the left. Follow this track round into the Chalamain Gap.

The view from the shoulder of the hill is quite spectacular, but for an even finer sight, climb the hill to the left. The best place for the ascent is just before the start of the crags in the gap, and be sure to follow the same route up and down. The summit cairn, at 2,580 ft., provides a grandstand view of the best features of this area. Braeriach commands the far side of the Lairig Ghru which, from this lofty platform, seems to be an impossible and impassable chaos of glacial banks and dykes. Rothiemurchus is a green and pleasant land, and the Kincardine hills bound the Queen's Forest on the right.

It is rather like a fine necklace: the separate stones of which, however beautiful individually, look far better when they are strung to-gether. As with jewels, so with mountain country. There is really no need to climb the hill to see all this, but the hill is there, the ascent is easy, and it enables the scenery to be enjoyed as a whole, rather than as a series of disconnected gems.

The Chalamain Gap cries out for photographs, or, better still, a video camera. It is the epitome of all that is rocky and rugged, and a viewpoint just inside the Gap will look straight through Ryvoan to Rynettin, with an unimaginable rocky chaos in the foreground. The way on is over this chaos, and care is needed when negotiating the pass.

The return path over the moor rejoins the outward route at the cairn on the escarpment, just below the reindeer fence.

WALK 3
A DAY FOR BIRDWATCHING

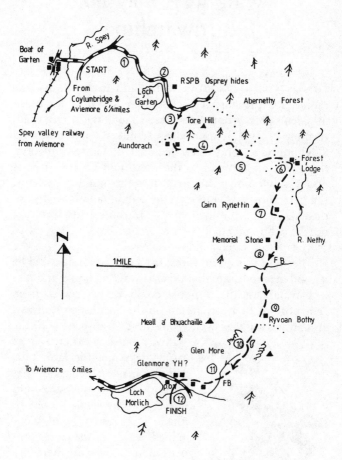

Walk 3: A Day For Birdwatching

THIS IS NOT A CIRCULAR WALK, and transport will be required to the start at Loch Garten, and from the finish in Glenmore. From Aviemore, follow the B970 road, turning N at Coylumbridge. About six miles beyond Coylumbridge, and after the Boat of Garten junction, there is a minor road to the right, and Loch Garten is about a mile down this road. It is the base for, perhaps, the best known RSPB reserve in Britain, and is well sign-posted. Across the loch, the Kincardine Hills form the northern boundary of Glen More, and the walk back to there is about twelve miles.

Because it is all on forest tracks or roads, it could be a good idea to forget that this is a walking book, and hire a bicycle. Another option could be to travel from Aviemore to Boat of Garten on the Strathspey Railway, and either walk or cycle from there. The snags with the railway are the restricted oper-

Osprey

ating days and the late start, but you may well consider that the considerable pleasure and nostalgia of travelling on one of the lovingly restored and main-tained trains is adequate com-pensation. However, there are all sorts of possibilities – use the OS map and some imagination.

It is well known that Loch Garten is the home of the ospreys, which settled down here in the 1950s, after an absence of half a century. Many pairs have been reared since then, and each year they return to Strathspey to breed. The most famous site is down a track on the E side of the loch, and a special hide serves the burned and blasted pine which is festooned with barbed wire for the protection of a pair of birds. There is adequate car-parking, and there are some way-marked walks around the loch.

Carry on along the road, and turn right at the first junction, past the settlement of Aundorach and Torehill Cottage. At a left bend in the road, where a forestry road goes off to the right, turn SE, down the forest road, and follow it, at first SE, and then almost due E, until just short of Forest Lodge and the River Nethy. The whole of the woodland here is now owned and administered by the RSPB, and it is a veritable Paradise for birdwatchers.

The following list of local species is not at all exhaustive, it is merely an appetiser:

Black grouse, capercaillie, crested tit, siskin, crossbill, osprey, great spotted woodpecker, golden eagle, sparrowhawk.

Now turn right, almost due S, and follow the Ryvoan path past Rynettin, and out of the forest. The way goes past the Memorial Stone (to a young man killed in the 1914-18 war) and on past Ryvoan Bothy. There surely cannot be another mountain area with so many memorials and monuments in such a small compass. There are more than a dozen between Glen

Ptarmigan

Feshie and Loch Pityoulish, and a visit to each would make for an interesting walking holiday – just a thought.

From Ryvoan it is straight down the 'Yellow Brick Road' to Glenmore. This track was so dubbed by a walking companion many years ago, and the name seems particularly apt for this stony pink and yellow track. It is a way to and from the wilderness, just like the road in the once-popular song.

If time permits, take the track to the left, just after Ryvoan Bothy. After about half a mile there is a small pile of stones on the left, and a faint track leads down through the heather to some trees by a lochan. This is Loch a' Gharbh Choire, which is sometimes a breeding ground for black-headed gulls. The nests are usually on the tops of the stumps in the E end of the loch. This lochan is fished by a local osprey.

WALK 4
LOCH MORLICH

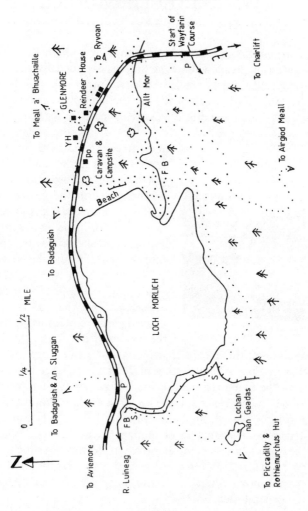

Walk 4: Loch Morlich

A circuit of the loch may seem to be just about the least interesting local walk. One side is bounded by the ski road, and forestry tracks flank two other sides. Only at the Allt Mor beach-head are there un-metalled paths expressly for walking on. As with many other things in this life, appearances can be deceptive: the walk is not devoid of interest and it is worth doing at least once. It is another piece in the geological jig-saw which has produced such a varied and attractive landscape. Take it slowly, and enjoy the wildlife and the views.

Loch Morlich

Loch Morlich is, apparently, a classic example of a kettle-hole. For those, the majority of normal folk, unfamiliar with the more esoteric jargon of the geologists, this means that it is a water filled depression that marks the final resting place of a very large lump of ice – the dying remnant of the last glacier in Glen More. Some 10,000 years ago the ice lump lay like a monstrous rotting tooth whilst the continuing thaw slowly embedded it in an aggregate of mud, sand, and gravel. When the ice melted the resultant cavity formed the loch. A crude description for a very complex process, but it does explain how it happened, and, hopefully, one can grasp the general idea.

It is amazing that geologists know all this because it happened such a long time ago, but it does explain the peculiar contours of the bottom of the loch which is generally shallow, except at the E end where a submarine cliff, with a slope of 1 in 4, falls 50 feet into the hole. The geological processes continue, and the edge of the cliff is advancing slowly westwards as the Allt Mor continually washes in a fresh supply of sand and gravel. Several acres of new beach have been added this century, and the rate of change is so rapid that differences can be noticed from year to year.

One day, perhaps, the loch will be no more; it will be filled up with detritus from the hills; and Cairngorm, perhaps, will be by then a mere shadow of its present self, and people will walk on it instead of up it.

The loch has an appeal of its own, and it occupies a picturesque and sheltered setting at the W end of Glen More. Surrounded by pinewoods, it nestles at the foot of the great northern corries of the Cairngorm massif, and it is an excellent place to observe Homo Sapiens as people busily enjoy their holiday in, on, or about the water. The red-gold sands provide a substitute sea-side for countless children - young, middle-aged and elderly.

The loch itself supports all sorts of quiet water sports – no noisy power boats and no water skiing – and the beach by the Allt Mor estuary is often thronged with optimistic anglers who stand like a row of mechanical toys as they hope – usually in vain – to hook an educated trout or pike. An occasional band of bewildered school-children, with glazed eyes and doodled clip-boards, follows the stream and an anxious teacher in search of O, A, or Higher level excellence – at least they will know all about kettle holes. The country is big enough to absorb them all, and the surrounding woods and marshlands provide plenty of scope for the nature-loving walker or idler.

The best times for a walk here are early or late in the day, and early morning has the edge so far as birdlife is concerned. Deer, both red and roe, seem to be seen more often in the late evening, although they are often all over the place just after dawn in late spring. It is appropriate to mention here that deer watching is an activity not normally associated with this kind of walking. It usually involves a lot of patient waiting, in the middle of the night, in a particular spot which deer are known to frequent.

Park by the Norwegian Stone in Glenmore, cross the road, and go through the caravan/camp site to the lake shore. There is a large, clean, attractive, very sandy, and extremely popular beach at this end of the loch. Follow the shore-line to the left, to the Allt Mor estuary. The area of beach here is growing all the time. The actual entry point into the loch can be seen to vary from year to year, which is geology in action. To the layman it is about as exciting as watching paint dry.

Go to the footbridge, upstream to the left, cross to the other bank, and follow the stream down to the shore again. There is a marked change of atmosphere here, and this part of the loch is a quiet, shallow and reedy bay that looks very 'pikey' to any fisherman. The land here is often under water in the cold half of the year, and even in summer it can be a bit swampy. Follow the shore-line, at first by the water's edge, and then through the woodland to a point where a path goes steeply uphill to the left. This leads onto a forest road that goes round the back of the loch, and the open aspect to the west, over the loch, is a good place from which to see some wonderful sunsets. This is also a good place to see wigeon, which seem to favour this quiet bay.

The view to the left is rather depressing following the virtually clear felling of large tracts of alien conifers. Cheer up: this is the beginning of a scheme to regenerate the Caledonian forest hereabouts, and it will be a pleasant woodland again in about fifty years.

Go right, along the forest road, which here runs high above the loch. The tree clearance has opened up splendid views across to the Kincardine hills. As the cleared area comes to an end the track starts to descend quite steeply through a close-planted mature woodland. Just before the deer fence, which marks the boundary with Rothiemurchus Estate (NH959089), another forest road cuts back to the left.

Follow this road uphill through a woodland of closely planted Scots pine, with the occasional downy birch for contrast. The track is of closely packed pink granite gravel, which is crunchy underfoot and makes for pleasant walking. It contours around the foot of a sizable knoll for about a quarter of a mile to where a sign points to Serpents Loch, on the left.

The picnic table by the loch is set in a little glade, and it is used not just by humans. The ground here is literally completely covered with the debris of pine cones left by banqueting squirrels. It is an idyllic spot, not to be missed.

Retrace the path back to the Rothiemurchus fence, and cross the stile - there is a special gate for dogs. It will be obvious that the fence is not just a boundary between two estates, it also separates two entirely different forms of woodland. The pleasant but rather formal planting of the Forestry Commission is here replaced with a more open and quite delightful natural tract of old forest. The road may be rougher, but there is more sky – and more sun – and the Scots pines are joined by juniper scrub and a lot more silver and downy birch.

The loch can be seen again, over to the right, and do keep a an eye on the sky – this is a favourite locale for fishing osprey. At the junction with the gravel road to Rothiemurchus Lodge, the route is followed to the right, to the Bailey Bridge crossing the Luineag at its out-flow from the loch. The way back to Glenmore follows the motor road, but that is not as bad as it may seem. There is always a pleasant grass verge to walk on, and there are many diversions by the loch and away from the road.

This is a basic walk of about four miles, but there is a veritable maze of paths and tracks behind the beach at the E end of the loch, and it is fun to use the Ordnance map and make up your own private routes. They can cover a seemingly endless variety of new forest clearance, old woodland, loch side, stream side, meadowland, scrub land and marsh land.

There are opportunities here for observing almost every type of life, and subjects range from humans, arguably at the top of the animal kingdom, down to tiny wood mites, which are almost certainly at the bottom. Interesting woodland birds abound, and water fowl and plant life are abundant. Or just sit on a log and think; but do be wary of the wood ants – they bite like mad. Above all, do not sit on an ant hill – yes, it has happened, and they can seem inviting if you haven't seen them before.

Glenmore is a tiny and unpretentious hamlet at the NE corner of the loch. It comprises a Post Office-cum-Café-cum-General Store, a Youth Hostel, the Reindeer House, the Forest Enterprise Centre, and a chapel – all welcome and all welcoming for a good sing on a summer Sunday evening. There is also a group of foresters houses nearby. In the appropriate seasons the resident population is augmented by the transients at the Youth Hostel, on the caravan/camp site, and in the few B&B houses. These are often people who came one week for a week and wanted to stay on without really knowing why. They all went home, of course, but only after developing a tendency to keep coming back year after year.

Glenmore is a perfect compromise because it is relatively close to the fleshpots of Aviemore, but is sufficiently remote to be blissfully quiet between tea-time and breakfast-time. It is very close to the mountains, and is an ideal place for almost any sort of outdoor holiday. One wonders why the Aviemore Centre was not built here instead – perhaps the planners got it right for once?

The ambience is overwhelmingly one of peace and tranquillity, which rubs off on the visitors. People who, at home, would hurry by without a glance, are inclined to pause and discuss the weather – inevitably, the fishing – always so-so, the walking – never too strenuous, or

almost anything remote from the monotony of their normal – but seemingly all too abnormal – everyday world.

If it sounds like some primitive heaven or haven in
the Highlands, be assured that it is, and we all love it for
simply being here.

WALK 5
THE LAIRIG GHRU

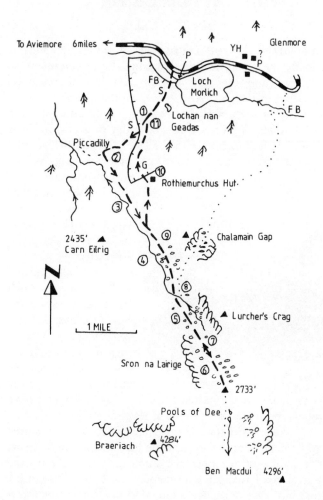

Walk 5: The Lairig Ghru

THE SHAPE OF THE LANDSCAPE in these highlands is mostly the result of glacial action. The mountains were sculpted and the valleys excavated by the relentless grinding of the ice. Frost, snow, wind and water continued the process, and the result is a wild and romantic countryside. A great ice-gouged valley runs N from Blair Atholl to its junction with the Dee at White Bridge near Braemar. The northward continuation of the valley towards Aviemore is the Lairig Ghru, which transects the Cairngorms' highest peaks.

Lairig Ghru

This walk, starting and finishing by Loch Morlich, goes to the top of the pass and traverses some of the most rugged and most beautiful mountain country in Britain. The scenery is dramatic in the extreme, the distance is about twelve miles, and the walk will take at least six hours.

Take the ski road from Aviemore to the picnic area and car park at the foot of the loch (NH958097). Cross the Bailey bridge over the Luineag, and walk up the gravel road towards Rothiemurchus Lodge. The track that branches to the left soon, after the start, is the forest road that goes behind the loch and back to Glenmore. Ignore this and carry straight on, heading for the volcano-like cone of Carn Eilrig, which is dominant in the background. After about a mile, there is a fork in the road, and the right branch is followed towards Piccadilly.

Cross the deer fence at the stile with the dog flap by it. As the fence starts to bear off to the left it takes the new plantings with it, and the path goes ever more deeply into the old woodland and the stony road is forgotten as the enchantment of the forest takes hold. The

Roe Deer

path starts to go quite steeply downhill, and just after this two sylvan glades open up to the left; tread lightly and quietly now, for the glades are a favourite haunt of deer. When the wind is southerly and there is no one else about it can be most rewarding in this spot. If a browsing roebuck senses an intruder and barks, bark back from cover, and wait. Roe deer are quite inquisitive, and he might come over for a closer look.

The track continues to a cross-roads in the forest where there is a large National Nature Reserve cairn and, maybe, a sign pointing to Braemar. Piccadilly was, at one time, a most important junction. The Lairig track continued N to cross the Luineag by a pine-log bridge to Coylum Bridge and beyond, and a branch of the track, by the river, went E to the Medicine Well, Fuaran Raoin Fhraoich, (OS Rinraoich), which drew visitors from as far afield as Braemar.

The E-W road which crosses here is the old Thieves Road, used by the caterans of Lochaber on their forays into the fat cattle lands of Banff and Moray. Apart from the road surface, the country here is probably little altered since those times, and it should be savoured, for this is the oldest, and the largest, and the least changed remnant of the ancient natural woodlands of Britain. It is a place to be cherished, and it is a privilege just to walk here.

Take the track S towards Braemar. The surrounding woodland becomes progressively more beautiful as the path ascends, and Carn Eilrig is prominent to the right, across the valley of the Allt Druie. Note the considerable variation in the trees; not in the species, for they are all Scots pine, but in their shapes, sizes and ages. This is a living woodland, and regeneration seems to be good, despite the deer. Note also the signs of devastation here and there, which is the legacy of past storms, and remember, when 70mph gales make the headlines in the Southron press, that winds of more than 100mph are not uncommon here. The fallen trees provide shelter and sustenance for a wide variety of insects and fungi, so it is not all bad news.

As the woodland starts to peter out the scenery all about is an assault on the senses, so theatrical are the views. Behind, below, and to the right, the river courses through a gorge clothed densely in variegated woodland. Ahead, the sheer-walled pass between the mountains beckons or threatens, depending on the weather.

This is the fringe of the forest, and as the path climbs higher onto the open moor the woodland clings to the shelter of the deeply cut valley sides, and in the more sheltered depths the delicate foliage of the birches provides a welcome change from the ubiquitous pine and juniper. Across the valley, the E flanks of Carn Eilrig are often speckled with grazing deer. The general beauty of the place was recognised by those great artists the Ordnance Survey cartographers, and the old map of 'Aviemore and the Cairngorms' had a striking drawing of a cock capercaille against the background of a delightful and intriguing river valley. The viewpoint for this scene is about NH940067, just to the side of and immediately below the path.

To the south, as the trees are left behind, one of the most photographed mountain scenes in Britain takes the breath away. Precipitous mountain sides rise above a bewildering foreground jumble of glacial banks and dykes, which are all that remain of a vast glacial lake that once covered this region. The path keeps to the main hillside, and stays high above the valley floor to the left of the stream. As it descends to meet the stream, a prominent knoll rises on the right, opposite the junction with a path emerging from the Chalamain Gap. Older maps identify it with the Sinclair Hut, but this was dismantled some years ago.

For some years now there has been a policy of removing the high level shelters and refuges in these hills. The intention has been to save lives, because parties were planning winter expeditions that depended on overnight stays in the shelters. On several occasions the shelters were not found in bad weather, and fatalities resulted. Sinclair Hut was removed because it was too near to Aviemore, and it became a notorious venue for week-end revellers – thus negating its real purpose. The path behind the knoll is the 'easy' way up Braeriach, via Sron na Lairige.

It must be admitted that the way from here to the top of the pass can be rather trying. The route is over the top of glacial debris laid down during successive melts, and while the resultant gravel beds appeal to the eye from a reasonable distance, they do not provide an ideal path. The way goes gently uphill, following the stream, and frequently changing course to avoid the largest boulders. There must have been a considerable deterioration in the condition of the track during the last hundred years, and it now seems inconceivable that it was once used regularly by young girls travelling from Rothiemurchus to sell eggs in Braemar. It was also used by shepherds, herding sheep to markets in the south. Nowadays it would test the abilities of a mountain goat!

After a seemingly endless struggle, the view from the cairn at the summit of the pass is adequate compensation for the uphill grind, and the eye travels down the line of the infant river towards the Linn of Dee, with Cairn Toul and Devils Point to the right, and the steep W slopes of Ben MacDui on the other hand. A few hundred yards downhill from the summit cairn, the Pools of Dee are worth a visit. There are usually four pools, and it is said that they never freeze. They are also much deeper than they look - so be warned if tempted to cool off. The pools are often thought to be the source of the Dee, but this is at the Wells of Dee, high up to the right near to the summit of Einich Cairn.

Retrace the route to about a mile beyond the junction with the Chalamain track, where a track bears off to the right, signposted to Rothiemurchus Lodge (NH950057). Follow this track to the NE, round the flank of Castle Hill. The way is stony, sometimes boggy, and winds gently, but relentlessly, upwards for about half a mile to Rothiemurchus Lodge. The Lodge is a large and comfortable hostel maintained by the Army for military personnel training or holidaying in the area. The gravel service road for the lodge is followed, downhill all the way, to the start point by Loch Morlich.

Spare some time to linger by Lochan nan Geadas: a serene and little-visited oasis fringed with handsome trees, and where oyster catchers and goosanders nest on an island. In the appropriate season this is good place to see goldeneye. This place is devoid of litter, which nowadays makes a refreshing change.

An alternative return is via the Chalamain Gap. Refer to the notes and sketch map for walk 2 and, at the junction with the track at the prominent knoll (NH959036), take the path which goes uphill and through the gap. Follow the track across the moor to the hairpin bend on the ski road. Go down the road to Glenmore, and along the lochside to the car park. This variation will extend the walk by about two miles, and will add about an hour to the time.

Wayfaring

Even in this mountain wonderland it is possible to be stuck for something to do. The cloud may be down; the tops may have lost their appeal on a cold day; it could be that the beach is 'out' on a sizzlingly hot day... whatever the reason, it just seems that nothing in particular appeals. This is the ideal time to try a spot of wayfaring. It has been described as orienteering without the sweat, and it is certainly a forest walk with a difference. Another advantage of wayfaring is its flexibility. The course can be tailored to suit one's exact requirements: from an hour's amble at one extreme, to a full and strenuous day in the forest at the other.

There is a wayfaring course in the Queen's Forest, and a cheap Wayfaring Package can be bought from many outlets in the area, including the Forest Enterprise Centre and the shop in Glenmore. The main components are an excellent map of the Queen's Forest, some general notes and information about wayfaring, and suggestions about how to get started. Equipped with this map and a compass it is possible to wander about in the forest without using any of the forest-walk paths. In fact, the basic pack provides all that is necessary for a wide variety of forest walks. If you really want to learn to read a map and use a compass, this is the ideal way to do it.

To give some sense of purpose go to the point where the master map is displayed – this varies with the re-aforestation programme. The map has all the wayfaring controls marked on it. The controls are wooden posts with a distinctive symbol and code letters painted on the top, and the idea is to mark-up your own map with the locations and numbers, and then seek them out on the ground. Complete instructions come with the map. It is really orienteering, but a lot more relaxed.

Although it is not supposed to be competitive – that is normally a feature of orienteering – wayfaring is an ideal basis for a family 'fun' day-out in the woods. If you go round the controls and keep a note, you can send off and get a diploma from the Inverness Orienteering Club. It looks impressive.

It is a different world in the forest, and it isn't just a lot of trees. There are rare flowers and birds, dramatic ravines and a secret lochan. There are no routes - you make your own – and there is a lot of quiet satisfaction and a real sense of achievement to be had in navigating from point to point in what is, after all, a quite bewildering terrain. Be prepared for funny looks from the ordinary walkers you will see from time to time as you burst out of the forest, cross one of the tracks, and disappear into the undergrowth on the other side. And if you dress discreetly and move quietly you could see a lot of unusual wildlife.

Cairngorm Weather Station

An interesting and varied alternative is to try one or more of the Pathfinder routes in the Rothiemurchus Estate. Pathfinding is essentially the same as Wayfaring, but there are three different levels: the 2½ Scout, the 5½ mile Traveller, and the 7½ mile Explorer. They use the extensive network of paths and quiet roads within the boundaries of the estate, and cover an extensive, varied and fascinating range of countryside.

The Pathfinder pack can be purchase from the Visitor Centre at Inverdruie, where the master map is also to be found. Although somewhat more expensive than Forest Enterprise's wayfaring pack, the Pathfinder set is worth the extra money.

Background

THE CAIRNGORMS ARE UNIQUE amongst British mountains in terms of altitude, of climate, and of scale. This is not a region where the inexperienced fell walker can wander about at will with impunity; walkers need to acquire a fair degree of high-level wisdom, and need to know their limitations on the good days and the bad. 'High-level' in this context refers to altitude, not to intellect. Also, it helps to have a balanced attitude to the countryside, and an appreciation and understanding of one's surroundings. Walks on the mountains are measured in hours, not miles, and this is a most important distinction, for which there are good reasons.

Away from the chairlift, whatever the season, the plateau and its surroundings are still quiet and unspoilt. Most of the walking is over trackless ground, and sheer size ensures that this area will long remain one of the last outposts of wilderness in Britain. It is a land of unexpected and unique delights for those who are prepared to look for and linger over the unusual. It is also a place of unexpected dangers, and the absence of prominent small-scale features can make it a bewildering place to be in fog or a sudden white-out.

More so than anywhere else in Britain, walks on or about these summits tend to be governed by the weather, and should be planned accordingly. Do bear in mind that temperature falls by about 4° F per thousand feet with increasing altitude, and wind speed (and therefore wind-chill) also increases with height. In practical terms this means that a late spring day, with a valley temperature of 60 degrees and a 10mph wind, will produce a cold day, with gale force winds and a risk of snow showers on the summit plateau. Always be equipped to cope with extremes of weather, and if things take a turn for the worse it is prudent to beat a hasty retreat to lower levels.

It is worth knowing that the most arctic conditions in Britain have been recorded about here: minus 17 degrees F (49 degrees of frost!) in the winters of 1895 and 1981, and a wind speed of 144mph was recorded in March 1964. Similarly high winds occurred here in 1987, during the great storm, when winds of lower speed devastated much of southern England and wreaked havoc in Rothiemurchus forest.

Weather is always the dominant factor, and this means that it is hopeless to have a set plan for a few days holiday. Keep a number of options open, and if a long trip is planned and a good day dawns, then do it, and don't put it off until tomorrow. This is not to say that the weather is always bad or always variable, far from it. It is common to have long spells of good and settled weather. These are most likely to occur in late spring and early autumn, which are also periods when insects (midges, that is) are least troublesome, and when there is not much snow. In early summer it is sometimes almost tropical, and the long days, with twilight extending almost to midnight, can provide gloaming walking of an almost magical quality.

There can be quite dramatic extremes during a single day, and the Information Centre in Aviemore once displayed two photographs which demonstrated this quite vividly. One showed scantily clad holiday-makers enjoying the warm April sunshine by Loch Morlich. The other depicted ice-trimmed walkers sorting-out a compass bearing in a blizzard of arctic intensity on the Cairngorm plateau some three thousand feet above. Both photographs were taken on the same afternoon. In fact, it is not at all unusual to have a white-out on Cairngorm summit on mid-summer's day. You have been warned!

In this region the general weather forecast is not much use, and it is always wise to get a local weather forecast before setting out for the hills. A forecast is always displayed by the Day Lodge of the chairlift, and at the Rothiemurchus Visitor Centre at Inverdruie. The Met. Office supplies information for Mountaincall: 0891 500 442, and there are many other telephone-based forecasts.

WALK 6
THE SHEPHERD OF GLEN MORE

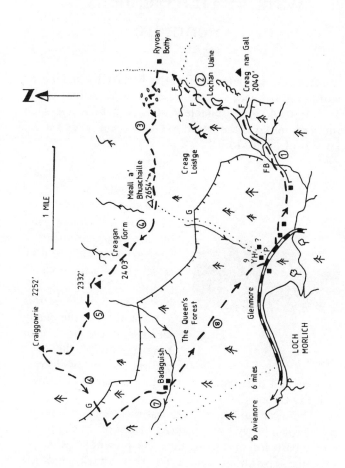

Walk 6: The Shepherd of Glenmore

THIS A GOOD WALK for the first day in the hills, and it provides extensive views of the main physical features of the area. It would be reasonable to allow about five hours for the walk, or six if the return to Glenmore is made via the far side of Loch Morlich.

Ryvoan Bothy

There is a small car park between the Youth Hostel and the Forest Enterprise Centre in Glenmore (NH970098), and on the adjacent green a large glacial erratic boulder is set in a small area of paving. This is the Norwegian Stone, which is a memorial to the many members of the Norwegian Kompani Linge who lived and trained in this district, and died on operations against the Germans in occupied Norway during the last war.

The most famous of these was the Telemark Raid on the German heavy water plant, the story of which provided the basis for an exciting film. The present youth hostel was the operations centre for that attack, and the Norwegian Hostel, between here and the new Glenmore Lodge, was built on the site of the commando barracks.

There is a timeless air about this striking memorial, and it is refreshing to see that somebody still cares – there are always fresh flowers at the base of the stone.

Turn left out of the car park and follow the left fork in the road past Reindeer House, the back of the foresters houses and follow the road towards Glenmore Lodge. This modern building has taken the name which rightly belongs to Loch Morlich Youth Hostel, the old hunting lodge of the Dukes of Richmond and Gordon.

A. Wainright pointed out that feet are always the last things to tire when traversing fell and moorland. Conversely, they are always the first things to tire when walking on Tarmac, and the truth of this assertion will be apparent in the first half mile or so if you walk on the road. Take heart, for most of the way the road has a foresters scrape on the left hand side, and there is plenty of interest in a walk along here. There are milk-, butter-, louse- and other worts, and there are newts in the puddles. Where do they come from, and where do they go? The newts, that is.

The road is gated just by the Lodge, and there is parking for about a dozen cars - please do not block the gateway. Beyond the gate there is a rough forest road and a complete change in the character of the country. The rough ground, now cleared of the serried ranks of alien conifers, is replaced by a much more open and interesting landscape. The foreground is dotted here and there with small Scots pines, which are some of the few survivors of the old Caledonian forest. They favour the low mounds of the drumlins, which were left behind when a large glacial lake emptied through Ryvoan.

The trees grow high up the flanks of Creag Loisgte and Creag nan Gall, which appear to form the walls of the pass immediately ahead. The tree line here is well above the

1,500 foot contour normally held to constitute the maximum altitude for successful tree growth in Britain. This is mainly because of the sheltered nature of the site, but because of poor soil fertility and the very short growing season at great heights, the trees, while very old are very small.

Continuing on the Ryvoan track, about half a mile on, on the right, An Lochan Uaine is in a dramatic setting backed by rugged screes and the trees of Creag nan Gall. The 'Green Lochan' is so called because the complete lack of marine vegetation, coupled with microscopic flakes of mica in the water, makes it reflect the colour of its rocky bed. Sometimes the water close inshore looks like custard, and this is caused by the accumulation of pollen from the surrounding pine trees.

Further on still, just about where the track starts to rise, a junction to the right is the way to Strath Nethy and the Lairig an Laoigh (the Pass of the Calves). Ignore this path and carry on to where, at the top of the rise, a corrugated iron roofed stone building is set in about five acres of lush grassland. This is Ryvoan Bothy, once a smallholding, but now a shelter maintained by the MBA. It is also the start point for the steep climb uphill. Inside the bothy there is adequate emergency accommodation for a snowy night. There used to be a visitors book, which made amusing and interesting reading, but the writing of obscenities, and other moronic malpractices, have resulted in its removal during the summer months. What a sad commentary on our times, and on some of the people who now come here.

From the door of the bothy a well used track heads roughly NW up the hill. During the climb, do pause from time to time to look back. A glorious panorama slowly unfolds and the ground, which at bothy level seems to be just a waste of scrub and heather, is seen to be an undulating country of glacial debris with numerous ravines, streams and small lochans. The mouth of Strath Nethy is seen, between Mam Suim and An Lurg, and the Lairig an Laoigh climbs into the distance before disappearing behind Bynack More.

There is a short but steep section which might require the use of hands as well as feet, but the gradient soon eases and it is then an easy walk to the summit. And wasn't it all so very much worth while?

From the summit shelter of Meall a' Bhuachaille there is, on a fine day, a superb and extensive view. To the N lies Abernethy forest with the Lochindorb moors beyond. To the NW, the whole of Strathspey is displayed, with the mighty Ben Wyvis range in the far background. The Monadhliaths are to the W and, in the SW, Loch Alvie and Loch an Eilean lie beyond the broad sweep of Rothiemurchus. Carn Eilrig stands alone, dividing the ways into Glen Einich and the Lairig Ghru. To the S, and immediately below, there is the Queen's Forest, with Loch Morlich set like a sapphire in a cushion of velvety green. The Cairngorm massif dominates the background to the S and SW, and there are excellent but distant views into the great corries. In the E, away to the left beyond Strath Nethy, the Bynacks look like a stranded and petrified prehistoric beast.

In late spring and early summer it is worth lingering for a while on the N slopes near to the summit to examine some of the rarer alpine plants which seem to thrive about here. Pride of place must go to wild, or creeping azalea (Loiseleuria procumbens), which is Britain's only native member of the Rhododendron family. Its tiny five petalled pink flowers stand out against the glossy dark green foliage in the warm sunshine, and provide a feast of nectar for pollinating insects. Superficially similar, but on close examination quite different, moss campion (Silene acaulis) provides an harmonious contrast of paler pink and green.

An obvious path strikes downhill W from the summit. Ignoring the track to the left at the first col, which is a quick way back to Glenmore, bear right and carry on along the ridge for the ascent of Creagan Gorm. The track along the ridge is carefully graded, and all the large stones have been moved to the sides. This must have been a dreadful and immensely tedious labour which was carried out by past generations for the convenience of Victorian sportsmen. It is an old stalking road, and there is still plentiful evidence of the presence of grouse and deer.

On the col between Creagan Gorm and the next peak, a massive erratic of pink Cairngorm granite is in marked contrast to the pale grey granulite all about, and provides welcome shelter for a rest. The next peak has no name, and there is a further minor summit before the track finally bears off again, uphill to the right, to Craiggowrie. This is effectively the end of the ridge, and there is now a definite path down, blazed through the heather and marked by concrete posts. There is a way through the forest fence, and a track leads to the old forest settlement of Badaguish. After many years of neglect this is now enjoying a new lease of life as a childrens holiday camp, supported by the Lord's Taverners.

It is a sign of the times that many muddy stretches mar this route, and that a once wild, but still exhilarating, hilltop walk is routinely punctuated by painted marker posts for the guidance of walkers. These may be easier to maintain than the usual piles of stones, but they hardly enhance the landscape, and they have about as much charm as the fence posts they so closely resemble.

Beyond Badaguish the track forks and, depending on

time or inclination, you must decide whether to take the long or the short way back. For the short route, take the left (E) track. To return by the longer way, take the good forest road to the right, and at the junction with the main road at the lochside turn right. Walk up the road to the loch, cross the Bailey Bridge, and follow the gravel road round the S side of loch Morlich and through the caravan site to the start point.

And the Shepherd of Glen More? Well, Meall a'Bhuachaille is Gaelic for the Shepherd's Hump, and the ridge is a dominant feature of the northern boundary of the glen.

WALK 7
BEN MACDUI

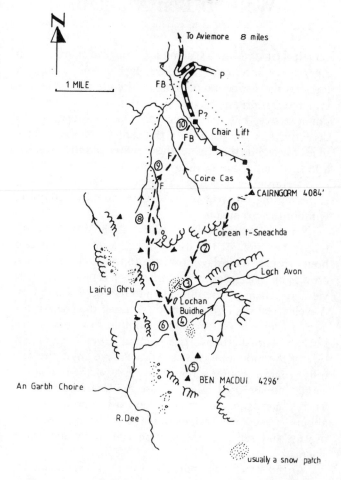

To Aviemore 8 miles

P

FB

1 MILE

P?

⑩

FB

Chair Lift

F

⑨

F

Coire Cas

▲ CAIRNGORM 4084'

①

▲

⑧

Coirean t-Sneachda

▲

②

Loch Avon

⑦

③

Lochan
Buidhe

Lairig Ghru

⑥   ④

▲
⑤ BEN MACDUI 4296'

An Garbh Choire

R.Dee

usually a snow patch

Walk 7: Ben MacDui

TO THE S OF CAIRNGORM summit the plateau culminates in a gently rounded hill. This is Ben MacDui which, at 4,296 feet, has the distinction of being the second highest mountain in Great Britain. Seen from Cairngorm, it is somewhat unimpressive, but the appearance, like the distance, is deceptive. As the eagle flies the summit is about three miles away, but there is no direct route, and the ascent is a long, if not arduous, undertaking. This is not meant to be off-putting, it is merely a statement of fact and, weather permitting, no visit to the region would be complete without this excursion.

The purists will want to walk it all the way, but common sense dictates the use of the chairlift to save two hours from a long day. From the top station, follow the crowds up to Cairngorm summit, which is worth it for the view, and then go carefully down to the top of Coire Cas. A well worn path goes from there along the edge of the corries, up above Aladdin's Couloir, towards Cairn Lochan. The alternative is a contour around the far (S) side of the mountain, which will not save any time. The other contour route, across the N face of the mountain, should not be used now because it is extremely rough. There is also landscape reclamation work in progress hereabouts. 'Landscape Reclamation' is a euphemism for tidying up and reparing the erosion caused by too many skiers.

At the start of the pull up to Cairn Lochan summit, bear off to the left and keep going vaguely uphill, following a faint track going SW to Lochan Buidhe. Do not be tempted down to the lower and apparently easier ground to the E. This is a region of small streams and often soggy rough ground, and all the lost height will have to be regained. The route from the lochan is marked by small cairns over rough grass and weathered granite gravel. There are some large snow patches that can linger into the early summer, and care is needed when crossing them. The snow is usually quite deep, the crust gets rotten by the end of May, and it is irritating and tiring to be forever breaking through. The trick is to walk on the old ski tracks, where the snow is more compact.

A false summit to the left should be ignored. Press sternly on, following the cairns on the old straight track, and the last rise will be breasted to reveal a well-worn path to the wide and airy mountain top. Once there, the trudgery of the approach will be forgotten, overwhelmed by the splendours of the views. There is a view indicator on a stone pillar, a little way to the W of the summit cairn. On

a good day the view extends for a hundred miles all round, over the boundless ocean of the hills, and it certainly encompasses rival Ben Nevis, 57 miles away to the W.

Immediately across the Lairig Ghru the foreground is dominated by Cairn Toul and Angel's Peak, with the Devil's Point to the S. There is a view into the enormous hanging valley of Coire Brochain, immediately below the summit cairn of Braeriach, and there is also a superb view of the depths of An Garbh Choire on the S side of Braeriach. The large snow field here is the nearest thing to a glacier in Britain, and some snow persists here all the year round. There is a local legend that the chief of Clan Grant will die within six months if this snow patch disappears. He last had cause to worry some thirty years ago, when only a very small patch survived. Since then it has grown larger year by year.

There are other legends too, and perhaps the most persistent is that of the Grey Man of Ben MacDui. James Hogg, the Ettrick Shepherd, mentioned the spectre about 200 years ago, and there have been many reported experiences since then. Not all can be dismissed as hysterical fantasies of disordered minds, and some of the reports have come from very distinguished mountaineers. Perhaps the best known is the 1925 testimony of Prof. Norman Collie, a professor of London University, and one of the greatest mountaineers of his era. He came off the mountain alone and terrified one day, convinced that something eerie was dogging his footsteps in the mist. Collie refused to go on the mountain alone after this.

There certainly seems to be something unusual about the summit area at certain times, and the reported sightings of a grey figure are too numerous to count. The rational explanation invokes a form of the Brocken spectre, and this is certainly not unusual here given the right atmospheric conditions. But that alone is an inadequate explanation for all the reported phenomena.

In late spring there are many snow buntings about, and these delightful little birds, which are supposed to be a rarity, will quite cheerfully scrounge crumbs from the weary walkers' sandwiches. Like many truly wild creatures, they have little fear of humans and sometimes literally get under the feet, so anxious are they to get their share of crumbs. The lower ground to the E, above Loch Avon, is a nesting area for the equally rare and equally tame dotterels.

To return, follow the route back towards Cairn Lochan, but just before Lochan Buidhe bear off to the left. The track follows the cliffs for about half a mile, and overlooks the Lairig Ghru. There are some very impressive views of Rothiemurchus. The way swings gently round to the N, along a shallow gully to the edge of Coire an Lochain, and from a break in the rocks a path goes steeply down inside the corrie. IF THERE IS THE LEAST VESTIGE OF SNOW ABOUT DO NOT USE THIS PATH. Instead, keep to the crest of the ridge, which provides a long and gentle descent down Lurchers Meadow towards the Allt Mor. During the descent work over to the right, and aim to bottom out just below the N rim of the corrie.

There is a way from here, over undulating ground, to the chairlift car park. This was the proposed route for the infamous road to Lurchers Meadow, which would have brought ski tows to this pleasant hillside. An altenative way is to continue down the ridge to the N. This ultimately connects with the Chalamain path, which can then be followed along the edge of the escarpment, by the reindeer compound, and across the Allt Mor bridge to the junction with the ski road by the car park at the big hairpin. Glenmore is downhill to the left and the chairlift car park is up the road to the right.

This is a long and often arduous walk, and in reasonable weather it will take at least six to eight hours. As always, leave note of your intentions before setting out, and any serious deterioration in the weather should be a signal to abandon the walk.

WALK 8
CAIRNGORM NORTH RIDGE

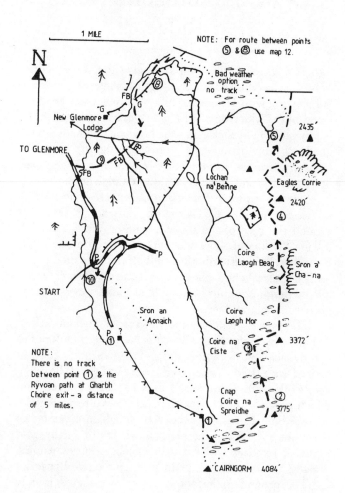

1 MILE

N

NOTE: For route between points ⑤ & ⑧ use map 12.

Bad weather option no track

FB

"G" G

New Glenmore Lodge

TO GLENMORE

FB

⑨

FB

⑧

2435'

⑤

Eagles Corrie

Lochan na' Beinne

2420'

④

Coire Laogh Beag

Sron a' Cha – na

P

P

START

⑩

Sron an Aonaich

Coire Laogh Mor

Coire na Ciste

③

3372'

NOTE:
There is no track between point ① & the Ryvoan path at Gharbh Choire exit – a distance of 5 miles.

P ?
①

Cnap Coire na Spreidhe

②

3775'

①

▲ CAIRNGORM 4084'

Walk 8: Cairngorm North Ridge

THIS IS A PLEASANT WALK for an off day and, if the chairlift is used, it has the added advantage of being mainly down-hill walking with only minor hills to climb. There are good views of the Kincardine Hills and Glen More, lower Strath Nethy and the Bynacks, and the braes of Abernethy to the north. A short detour may be made to the top of Eagle's Corrie, which has an impressive rock face, a resident pair of peregrines, and a fine collection of alpine flora.

Starting from the Ptarmigan Cafe there is no need to go to the summit of Cairngorm, instead, traverse left around the base of the summit cone on the N side, fol-lowing the line of ski-tow towers to the top of the ridge. From here it is virtually downhill all the way on a pleas-antly undulating high plateau. A zig-zag course will take in all the minor summits, and gives splendid views into the corries to right and left.

There are especially grand views from the high cliffs of Sron a'Cha-no that soar above the Nethy, and look out to the Bynacks – More and Beag. The enormous gully of Coire Dearg (Red Corrie), to the right of Bynack Beag is a spectacular sight from here. This is also a good place from which to study the Bynacks if it is intended to walk them at some time. Carriers of binoculars should look out for an eagle soaring in the thermals above Strath Nethy, and herds of reindeer and red deer can be seen sometimes, grazing on the high level plain between the two Bynacks.

The ground underfoot is mainly weathered granite gravel, with a sparse and broken mossy covering. There are outcrops of granite here and there, the uniform pink broken by blazes of pure white quartz, and the whole patterned with lichens in an array of muted colours. Bands of snow will lie late in the hollows, and watery patches look boggy but usually are not.

Unusual plants include wild, or creeping azalea, and the pink and white blossom in late spring forms colourful cushions amidst the general desolation of the near tundra. Notice also the ripple pattern of the ground: this shows the direction of the prevailing winds. The ridges run from NW - SE, and a 45 degree transect is a pretty accurate N-S line: this can be useful in a white-out, or if the clouds come down.

Instead of pressing straight on to the end, it can be both instructive and rewarding to spend some time exploring this delightful upland. The first objective, no doubt, will be the summit of Cnap Coire na Spreidhe, which beckons about a quarter of a mile due E of the Ptarmigan cafe. It is topped by a distinctive and eminently climbable tor, which rises from a jumble of long since detached boulders and slabs. The view from its little summit is quite sensational because the land to the E falls away sharply in an apparently sheer rock face.

Heading roughly N to the next summit, note how there is a fairly distinct edge to ridge, beyond which the ground falls away almost as a precipice. This is a relic of the glacial past that occurs about the 3,000 foot contour throughout the Cairngorms. It is a useful height indicator in conditions of poor visibility. This summit is a good place from which to look back towards Cairngorm, and along the face of the Nethy gorge to Beinn Mheadhoin and Ben MacDui.

Spectacular snow cornices often survive here into early summer, and add a touch more drama to the views. From the N around to the W, the panorama of distant mountains is remarkable. Ben Nevis can be seen on a good day, and Ben Eighe and Ben Wyvis are also often seen, providing a grand backdrop to the jewel of Loch Morlich immediately below.

Moving away from the ridge towards the NW, the ground falls away gently to the head of Coire Laogh Mor. Boulders become much more numerous, and so do the ptarmigan, which seem rather fond of this particular locality. In one way they seem more akin to pheasants than to grouse, and that is in their seeming reluctance to fly. Ptarmigan are not particularly shy birds, but it is difficult to get in really close, and they have an irritating propensity to be always behind the next rock. When a bird does take to the air it will do a quick cart-wheel, and then land not far away. It is possible to double-bluff them in the interests of a photograph.

Move N, back to the main ridge, which is followed to the end. The descent is quite steep, and a distinct path appears. Before descending do pause and look at the sheer face of the corrie ahead, and down into the depths of Strath Nethy to the right. This is a grandstand view of the intricate glacial deposits which demand so much effort when they are being negotiated on the ground.

The path drops down to a large and complex col, at the far end of which is the top of Eagle's Corrie, one of the outflow channels formed by melt water when a glacial lake burst its banks here some 10,000 years ago. The vegetation is more varied at this lower level, and the lichen, rushes and mosses of the high plateau are joined by grasses, cow- and crow-berries, and abundant heather. Look out for, but do not pick, the delicate white flowers of the cloudberry. A rarity here, this relative of the raspberry grows in abundance on the tundra of Scandinavia, where it is used to make a delicious jam.

A low hill to the left hides the view down to Glen More. In some of the peat scours about here there are exposed the gnarled and twisted roots and stumps of long-vanished large Scots pines. These remains of the old Caledonian forest, now preserved in the peat, grew here more than 2,000 years ago when the climate was very much warmer than to-day. They are about 500 feet above the present tree line. There is also evidence that the peat scours are frequented by deer: their tracks are all over the place, and it is not unknown to come across large herds here in the spring.

Eagle's Corrie is to the right, and it is worth making a digression down the obvious broad and gentle gulley. A stream soon appears, and this is followed to the head of the corrie. The ice-sculpted rock face is quite spectacular, to say the least, and a prominent rocky knoll provides a useful vantage point from which to view the antics of the resident birds. If the peregrines are about, they will have made their presence known in their usual extremely noisy way. There is a good selection of alpine flowers here in the spring, and it is worth lingering for a while. Return by the same route to the main ridge.

From this point some guides recommend a traverse to the left, down the flank of Creag nan Gall to the Ryvoan track. This involves the descent of a steep hillside, thick with deep heather and concealed boulders. It makes a trying, possibly hazardous, and unsatisfactory end to the walk. Instead, keep going N, and make for Eag a'Gharbh Choire, a rather obvious notch in the ridge ahead, which is another glacial overflow channel that goes through to An Gharbh Choire. Gharbh means 'rough', and the reason for the name will become apparent in good time.

At the entrance to the pass there is a sheepfold, and the way is not at all obvious. Keep to the left hand side and tread carefully: it would be easy to twist or break an ankle here. It is all rather like the Chalamain Gap: a chaos of tumbled rocks and boulders, albeit on a smaller scale. The route soon starts to descend quite steeply, and hands as well as feet my be needed for a little while, but the going is not too bad on the left hand side.

It is possible to circumvent the Eag and, if the prospect of its traverse does not appeal, climb up and around, away from the edge on the left hand side, and over the ridge that runs E from Creag nan Gall. Carefully descend the peaty and grassy slope into the corrie. It is steep but easy. In summer the corrie is the home of many ring ouzels, and they can be seen and heard around the rock walls of Mam Suim, high to the right. They look like white-bibbed crows, but are actually members of the thrush family, and are not particularly afraid of people.

The way down is rough at first, but the tumbled rock soon peters out and the path becomes less steep. There is a sheep track beside a small stream, and a tiny lochan and occasional pools. Fingerling trout can be seen here in the stream, which in places is only a few inches wide.

The corrie is quiet and still little visited, and it ends quite suddenly. There is a dead tree on the right, and the track climbs over the back of a low drumlin on the left. One pace further on is the 'yellow brick road' between Ryvoan and Nethy bothies. Looking back, there is little indication that the corrie exists at all, it is all so beautifully hidden by the drumlins which comprise its floor. A small cairn sometimes marks the entrance to the corrie, and Glenmore lies about three miles down the road to the left.

In good conditions it is possible to complete this walk in four hours from the Ptarmigan cafe. In the sunshine it is usual and sensible to make it last all day because of the many potential distractions.

DO NOT ATTEMPT THE DESCENT OF AN GHARBH CHOIRE IF SNOW IS LYING ON THE GROUND. In these conditions it would be better to traverse down the S flank of Creag nan Gall. Make for the corner of the deer fence (NJ001810), taking great care when crossing the very rough ground. Alongside the deer fence a steep and muddy path descends to the Ryvoan track, just S of the Green Lochan. The way is to the left for Glenmore.

WALK 9
CAIRNGORM CORRIES

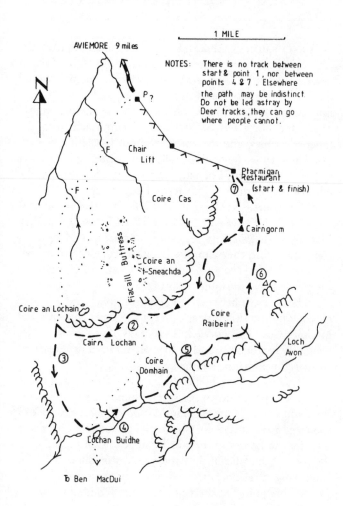

1 MILE

AVIEMORE 9 miles

N

NOTES: There is no track between start & point 1, nor between points 4 & 7. Elsewhere the path may be indistinct Do not be led astray by Deer tracks, they can go where people cannot.

P ?

F

Chair Lift

F

Ptarmigan Restaurant
(start & finish)
⑦

Coire Cas

▲ Cairngorm

Fiacaill Buttress

Coire an t-Sneachda

①

⑥

Coire an Lochain

②

Cairn Lochan

Coire Raibeirt

⑤

Loch Avon

③

Coire Domhain

④

Lochan Buidhe

To Ben MacDui

77

Walk 9: Cairngorm Corries

THIS EXCURSION COMPLEMENTS walk 8, and completes the traverse of the Cairngorm ridge. In fact, this walk, done in reverse, could be combined with walk 8, but this would make for a very long and strenuous day, and it is definitely not recommended. The whole idea of these walks is enjoyment, and not a test of stamina and endurance. The distance is 7 miles, and the duration about 3 or 4 hours.

The start is identical to walk 7, but instead of going off to the SW on Cairn Lochan, carry on uphill, following the edge of the corries on a fairly well defined track – this is a popular route. NOTE: IF THERE IS MUCH SNOW COVER WHEN WALKING HERE KEEP WELL AWAY FROM THE EDGE. Great snow cornices build up over the winter, and they can overhang the edge of the corries by several feet. They are never safe at any time, but they are particularly unstable in spring.

The contrast between the corries is great, and it is easy to see why the skiing development has been concentrated in Coire Cas. This corrie has no crags, and the slopes are generally reasonable, and it does often retain its wreath of snow right up to the summer.

Choire an t'Sneachda is the largest of the three, and the path goes up and down for several hundred feet following the undulations of the edge. Inside and below is a jumble of shattered rock. It is really two corries turned into one, and a little lochan nestles in the smaller hollow, well tucked in at the foot of the Fiacaill. In winter, headwall (shouldn't it be head-banger?) skiers practice their arcane skills in this corrie.

At this point, at the head of Coire Domhain, near to

the start of the Ben MacDui track, and where the ground falls away quite steeply to the S, the walker is confined to a fairly narrow isthmus, but it is perfectly safe, and little cairns show the way. The aptly named Goat Track goes steeply down into the corrie from near here, but that is not part of these walks. The rock buttress on Fiacaill an t'Sneachda is a magnet for rock climbers, and some dramatic photographs may be obtained from the track which passes by on the way to Lochan summit.

Choire an Lochain presents a magnificent spectacle from below, and is notable for the great rock face of red granite which holds snow until late in the season, and is the source of some big avalanches. From above there is not so much drama, and the track follows the corrie, around the edge of the gentle plateau, towards Lurchers Peak. In a hollow between Carn Lochan and the Lurcher (NH978028), a track goes S towards Ben MacDui. After about half a mile the track approaches the edge of the great trench of the Lairig Ghru, fairly near to the summit of the pass. The path then veers off towards the SE as it approaches Lochan Buidhe.

A stream flows out of the lochan, and the left bank is followed down to the cliff top, overlooking Loch Avon. Make sure that the camera still has some film: it will be needed here.

Because this is a gathering ground for many small streams, it can be quite wet here and there, but the soil is so sparse that it is never really boggy. This is dotterel country, and these rare and attractive wading birds are quite tame. Ptarmigan are found here, too, and a snowy owl has been resident in the area, on and off, for many seasons.

The 'done thing' from here is to traverse round to the left, following the edge of the Loch Avon trench, into Corries Domhain and Raibert. The reward for a lot of hard walking is a constantly changing vista of sublimely beautiful mountain scenery. The climb out of Coire Raibert is followed by a walk around the base of Cairngorm, on the S side, to the Ptarmigan Café.

WALK 10
THE BYNACKS

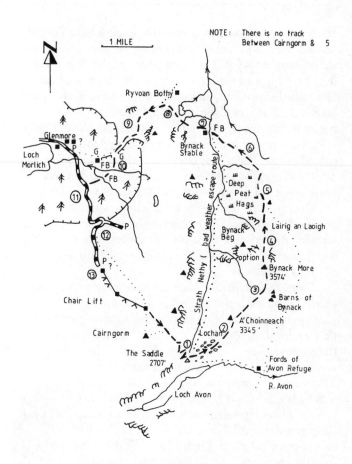

NOTE: There is no track
Between Cairngorm & 5

1 MILE

Ryvoan Bothy

⑨ ⑧ ⑦ FB

Glenmore ? ⑥

Loch Morlich

G
FB ⑩ G
FB

Bynack Stable

Deep Peat Hags ⑤

⑪

Bynack Beg

Lairig an Laoigh

⑫ P

option ④

P ?

Strath Nethy (bad weather escape route)

⑬ P ?

Bynack More 3574'

Chair Lift

③

Barns of Bynack

Cairngorm

② A'Choinneach 3345'

Lochan ①

The Saddle 2707'

Fords of Avon Refuge

R. Avon

Loch Avon

81

Walk 10: The Bynacks

TO THE AVERAGE WALKER used to the English Lake District, Snowdonia, and other mountains in the south, the Cairngorm massif will be a surprise, and at first sight it may be disappointing. Once on the plateau it is all rather like rolling downland, and it seems more like Sussex than Scotland, albeit on a somewhat grander scale. This is not meant to be disparaging, and old acquaintance breeds great affection, but the Bynacks are different, and they also offer something of a rarity – a genuine airy ridge walk. They also offer solitude, because very few walkers go beyond the great divides of Strath Nethy and the Loch Avon trench.

On the map this looks a very long walk, but it has always been found to be relatively easy, and in good weather it need take no more than seven hours from the top station of the chairlift, back to the car park at the end of the ski road.

From the Ptarmigan cafe contour round to the left, heading E to the top of the ridge, and avoiding the path to Cairngorm summit. Then go downhill to the right for a little way, heading roughly S for about a quarter of a mile in the general direction of Coire Raibert. The route then swings round to the SE, heading down towards the Saddle. This side of the mountain overlooks the Loch Avon trench, although the loch is hidden at this height. Away to the S there is a hanging valley with the sugar loaf shape of Derry Cairngorm beyond. In the little valley lies Loch Etchachan, one of the bleakest and remotest of all the lochs, which is frozen over for at least seven months each year.

The route drops down by the S side of Ciste Mhearad,

which can hold a lot of snow. The way down is not very obvious, and there is no path, but common sense will direct the sensible walker away from the large rock outcrops. There is a stream to cross, with a very large rock face to the right. Aim to pass below this, and there will be a choice of several deer tracks all making down towards the Saddle, which can be seen from here.

The Saddle is the watershed between the Nethy and the Avon, and it is in an idyllic setting. the mountain and valley scenery all about is unforgettable. In particular, the view along Loch Avon towards the Shelter Stone Crag is undescribably beautiful. The route from here is to the NE. Do not follow the obvious track, contouring around the hill to the E, because this goes to the Fords of Avon. Instead, strike firmly uphill over the sparse heather plentifully dotted with loose rock and boulders.

The gradient is steep at first, but the constantly changing views back over Loch Avon provide plenty of excuses for frequent pauses. There is a little lochan on the left if the correct route is followed, and the gradient soon eases as the first summit of A'Choinneach is reached. Carry on to the top at 3,345 feet, and pause at the summit cairn to look around. Munroists will realise that another summit can be ticked off on the list.

Ahead there is a broad plain, running N-S at about 3,000 feet, which is frequented by sheep, reindeer and red deer, and the blue or mountain hare is by no means uncommon. Large herds of hinds congregate here in the spring, and we have seen as many as 40 deer, adults and young, grazing and wallowing in the peat. They are very canny, and it is an unforgettable sight to see a large herd take off and away. Where they go to up here is a mystery, for they are not seen again that day.

Beyond the plain there is the W face of Bynack More,

and the summit ridge is studded with red granite tors. At the far side of the plain there are some large peat scours, and the route lies between these, and up the far hillside to the rightmost tors.

The ridge tors are the Little Barns of Bynack, and they are very large at close quarters. The rock is peculiarly stratified and bedded, and looks as though it has been fitted with a damp-proof course. The Barns of Bynack proper cannot be seen from the ridge, and it is worth detouring for a few hundred yards downhill to the the E to look at them.

Back on the ridge, an exhilarating walk leads to the

Shelter Stone Crag

3,574 foot summit of Bynack More. Do keep a look out for Ptarmigan, which are fairly common, quite tame, but a bit shy. The view from the ridge is quite spectacular, and the dominant feature in the S is the Loch Avon trench, backed by Shelter Stone Crag and Ben MacDui. Away to the SE is the Ben Avon massif, which is a knobbly and humpy high level tundra rather than a mountain. To the E the ground falls away quite sharply, and the Lairig an Laoigh (Pass of the Calves) can be seen snaking along, following the contours at the base of the mountain. Beyond this there is a confused mass of lesser hills disappearing into the distance.

It all looks barren but benign in the sunshine, but the winter brings a different climate, and even the Pass of the Calves has its dangers. Not all that long ago a party got lost in a white-out on this pass, but some of them were lucky: blundering off course along the Caiplich, they finished up in Tomintoul.

In the opposite direction the view is bounded by the N ridge of the Cairngorm massif. The cliffs are an impressive sight from here, and they form majestic precipices, plunging down into the depths of Strath Nethy.

Follow the ridge downhill to the end, where the descent is steep but safe. A digression to the left will encompass the top of Bynack Beag, and will take an additional hour. The OS map suggests a possible route down to the Nethy here, down the broad northern gully of Coire Dhubh, which separates the two Bynacks. This has not been tried yet, so it is only a possibility.

The walk continues from the foot of Bynack More, keeping to the higher ground and tracking to the N. Some years ago, when walking here, we heard a dog bark in the sky, behind and to the left. It wasn't a dog, of course, but an eagle objecting to the attentions of a peregrine falcon. For ten minutes we lay in the heather and watched an incredible sight. The falcon was contesting the eagle's incursion into its airspace, and had decided to see the eagle off. It pecked at the tips and trailing edges of the eagle's wings and also had a go at its tail, but all to no effect. Finally, the falcon flew under the tip of the eagle's wing and tried to tip it over. The big bird merely lifted a wing and changed its flight path. In the end it had enough, and turned and soared away, back up the Nethy towards Loch Avon. The falcon, honour satisfied, flew off to the E. It is incidents like this that really make the day.

Eagle

85

There is quite a variety of unusual wildlife to be seen in this area, and at various times on this walk we have come across the following: blue hare, red deer, reindeer, ptarmigan, red grouse, golden eagles, an osprey and a peregrine falcon. We have also seen two frogs on snowy ground at well over 3,000 feet. Unfortunately for the frogs they were on opposite sides of Strath Nethy.

Firmly resist the temptation to follow the apparently easier course to the NW. This leads into some enormous and impassable peat hags, and inevitably leads to back-tracking and a needless waste of time. The way now is to the N over the higher ground on gloriously firm and springy turf dotted with tussocks of moss campion. The Lairig an Laoigh track is soon reached, and this is followed down to Bynack Stable and the road back to Glenmore. Just before the gate at Glenmore Lodge a forest track goes off to the left and intersects the ski road by the Allt Mor car park. It is two miles uphill on the roadside verge to the chairlift.

WALK II
CRAIGELLACHIE NATURE RESERVE

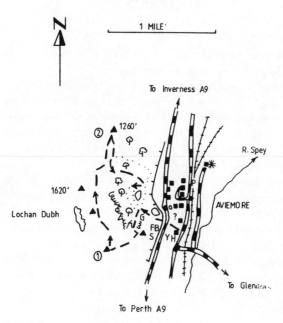

NOTE: The A9 footbridge is actually an underpass.

Walk 11: Craigellachie Nature Reserve

AT SOME TIME DURING any holiday there is a pressing need to go shopping. It may be that presents and post-cards have to be bought, or a map, or some new items of gear are required. It must be admitted that, from time to time, it is nice to get away from the rigours of the high hills. This walk provides an opportunity to do all these things without in any way compromising the idea and the spirit of a hill-walking holiday.

Craigellachie is the well wooded low hill with the sheer and craggy rock-face that provides such an impressive natural setting for the Aviemore Centre. It is this rock, and not the fishing town in lower Strathspey, that figures in the Grant motto 'Stand fast Craigallechie'. That Craigellachie endures is beyond doubt, and it is central to the little National Nature Reserve, which covers about 2 square miles of delectable low hill country to the W of Aviemore.

The reserve is notable on many counts, one of which is a resident pair of peregrine falcons. The reserve has a large area of birch scrub which is a habitat for many species of birds uncommon elsewhere in the area, for some reptiles and small mammals which are common but rarely seen, and for a variety of insect life that would be unusual anywhere, and which attracts naturalists from everywhere.

Go to the Tourist Information Centre in Aviemore and buy the leaflet describing the reserve. Then go and have a cup of coffee and read the leaflet. After the coffee it will be time to go to the reserve, which is approached through a corrugated iron tunnel under the A9.

It is strange that an area so delightful in itself is not over-run with other visitors. Not least of the delights of time spent here is that one rarely sees many other people. It is a little haven on the edge of the town, and most of the visitors encountered here seem to be specialist ornithologists, or other naturalists. This isolation is probably due to a combination of things, like the A9 which separates it from the town, general ignorance of the access tunnel's whereabouts, and lack of publicity.

Two paths lead to the tunnel, which was provided as the only access point when the A9 by-passed the town some years ago. One path runs from the main street, from a point between the Youth Hostel and a caravan site (NH894118). The other path starts from a bend in a road on the Aviemore Centre, near to the Badenoch Hotel (NH893123). It goes across the grass, following the fence, and picks up the other path near to the tunnel.

Once through the tunnel, go off to the right and follow the path through the woodland at the foot of the crag, and then to the left and up onto the duck-board staging, keeping to the higher level way. Near the first bend look for, and follow, a faint track that doubles back and goes uphill steeply through the woods to the left. This leads into a steep and narrow gully that goes straight up onto the ridge. it is easy scrambling all the way, but very rough and sweaty.

If this sort of scramble does not appeal, carry on along the long, upper, trail to where it meets a track which comes steeply downhill from the left, and obviously off the ridge. Follow this track up to the ridge, and then go left to the summit. At the top, the summit cairn is to the left, and this is the start of a pleasant little ridge walk offering superb views of the Cairngorms and this section of Strathspey.

At the end of the ridge, the path described above, goes down to the nature trail, and leads to some pretty rock and woodland scenery and a pleasant artificial lochan. The woodland is mainly birch scrub, which makes a pleasant change from the seemingly ubiquitous conifers elsewhere. there are many different butterflies and a riot of wild flowers, some of them very rare. There are stoats and a lot of lizards. It is worth while going round the rest of nature trail, using the leaflet obtained at the Information Centre.

Various walks are possible in the reserve, and some are shown on the map, you will soon create your own favourites, but the easiest course on a first visit is probably to follow a clockwise route around the nature trail on the finely graded path. This is constructed of gravel, stone slabs and duck boarding, depending on the terrain. It is beautifully done and maintained, and the 'viewpoints' are well chosen. There is nothing here of the artificiality so often evident on other nature trails. No numbered posts and set pieces, and apart from the path it is all as nature made it.

PLEASE DO NOT GO UP ONTO THE RIDGE IN APRIL AND JULY. These are critical months for the nesting peregrines, and they should be left undisturbed. During those two months there will be plenty of interest elsewhere in the reserve, and many opportunities to observe these magnificent birds from the best vantage point, which is at the foot of the crag.

Peregrine

Autumn is a particularly splendid season, and the reserve is especially beautiful then as the yellowing leaves,

90

when sunlit, provide a green, grey and gilded tapestry which is a vivid and unforgettable backdrop to the town. The quiet and contemplative stroller here will be rewarded with the sight and sounds of many unusual birds, moths, small animals and plants. It is all the more attractive for the marked contrast with the great pine forests nearby. Wander and wonder, and haste ye back!

This is a very easy day, and at the end there will be time to go into Aviemore, or Inverdruie and Coylumbridge, for a swim and some shopping before tea.

WALK 12
EAGLE'S CORRIE

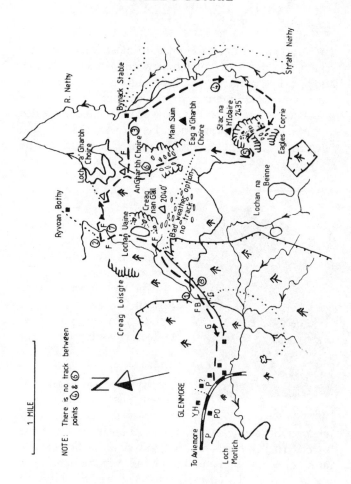

Walk 12: Eagle's Corrie

THE CHALAMAIN GAP IS familiar to most walkers in this region. It is the notable notch between Lurcher's Meadow and Creag Chalamain, and it provides a short-cut to the Lairig Ghru and Braeriach from Glenmore. Eagle's Corrie is an equally impressive but less well known feature which cuts into the Cairngorm N ridge between Strath Nethy and Glen More. A combination of traverses of Eagle's Corrie

Eagle's Corrie

and An Gharbh Choire provides an interesting and, at times, strenuous day out. Geologists in particular will find this a rewarding excursion because the walk encompasses a wide variety of glacial features.

The best approach is to park in Glenmore, or in the little lay-by by Glenmore Lodge – room for a dozen or so cars, and please do not obstruct the gate. Then take the Ryvoan track past the Green Lochan, and follow the track to the right at the

junction just before Ryvoan bothy. At the breast of the rise on this road there is a very good view of the rounded hump of Mam Suim and, up the valley to the right, there is a notable notch in the ridge. Mark it well, for this is the Eag a'Gharbh Choire, and the route passes through it on the return journey.

To the left, behind and below the drumlins that bound the road, Loch a'Gharbh Choire is a favoured breeding ground for gulls, and it is worth digressing towards the water's edge, to where the birds can be seen nesting in the old tree stumps, dotted about the lochan a few yards offshore. This lochan is dammed, and it was once used to collect logs from the forestry industry for floating down to the Spey. Nowadays it is a pleasant spot in which to spend a lazy day fishing, or observing odd plants like the insect-eating sundews and butterworts. Fishermen should note that the few trout here are a good size and quite wild. They are receptive to a March Brown fly, fished wet or dry depending on the conditions.

In a little while there is a signpost advertising the road to Braemar. Nearby, on the right, Bynack Stable, another of the mountain refuges or bothies, marks the entrance to Strath Nethy. The stark structure is well maintained if a little incongruous – it is made of corrugated iron – but the inside is rather squalid. One would have to be really desperate to spend a night here. Have a paddle in the icy stream by all means, but don't cross the bridge.

There is a route along a faint track along the W bank of the stream that starts from the banking behind the bothy. The track is not much used and is hard to follow in places, and it is also a bit soggy here and there. Persevere, and after about a mile, the way appears to be blocked by a low but steep bank that looks like the embankment of a dam (NJ024085). This is a moraine formed at the junction of two glaciers that once filled this valley. More importantly, it marks the entrance to the corrie.

It is worth pausing here for a look round. The enormous tree stumps, poking out of the peaty banks of the Nethy, are the last remnants of the forest that once covered the valley floor and hill sides. These remains, washed out from beneath the peat, are several thousand years old. This is a desolate spot, and very beautiful, and it is not unknown to come across one of the reindeer herds about here. The reindeer are very tame and very friendly in the spring. Don't be put off by their size, they are gentle beasts and seem to have an insatiable appetite for chocolate, which they will nibble out of your fingers. Stay away from reindeer if they are accompanied by calves, and always give them a wide berth in the autumn.

The way from here is up into the obvious valley to the right. There is a sort of track to start with, by a deeply cut rillet of a stream, and when the track peters out the best route is generally to be found on the left hand side. During the climb the sheer rock wall of Stac na h'Iolaire soars up to the right. It was carved by the force of the water when a glacial lake in Glen More burst its banks at the end of the last ice age. The frosts each winter break off more rocks to add to the stony chaos all about. It should be remembered that this is all part of a continual process which is grinding down the mountains to make the seaside.

During the ascent the going gets rougher, and the route passes over an incredible jumble of tumbled rocks. As the head of the valley closes in and there seems to be no going on, a way will be found up a steep but grassy slope to the left. Some scrambling is called for, but it is all quite safe. Near to the top there is a rock buttress on the left which supports a wide variety of alpine plants, including many different species of alpine lady's mantle.

The top is a good place to pause and look across to the rock face of Stac an h'Iolaire – the Peak of the Eagle – It really is an extraordinary sight, for a large segment of the mountain has been sliced off by the ice and water of a bygone glacier, and subsequent weathering has produced some magnificent screes. This is also a good place to sit and watch the antics of the resident peregrines, which roost in an old eagle's nest in the middle of the rock face. The corrie is also frequented by snow buntings, which can be identified by their mournful cry, and by ring ouzels, which arrive here early in summer.

Carry on upwards, out of the corrie, following the stream. The steep gradient quickly eases off, and the deer or sheep track continuing uphill to the left should be ignored. The way to the top of the ridge is through a little pass that goes W in the direction of Glen More.

In some of the peat scours about here there are exposed the gnarled and twisted roots and stumps of long-vanished large Scots pines. These remains of the old Caledonian forest, now preserved in the peat, grew here more than 2,000 years ago when the climate was very much warmer than to-day. They are about 500 feet above the present tree line. There is also evidence that the peat scours are frequented by deer: their tracks are all over the place, and it is not unknown to come across large herds here in the spring.

At this point the route joins the path descending from the N ridge of Cairngorm, and is continued as for the end of Walk 8. In good conditions it should be possible to complete this walk in four hours as a round trip from the car park in Glenmore. In the sunshine it is more sensible to make it last all day and enjoy the many potential distractions.

DO NOT ATTEMPT THE DESCENT OF AN GHARBH CHOIRE IF SNOW IS LYING ON THE GROUND. In these conditions it would be better to traverse down the S flank of Creag nan Gall. Make for the corner of the deer fence (NJ001810), taking great care when crossing the very rough ground. Alongside the fence a steep and muddy path descends to the Ryvoan track, just S of the Green Lochan. The way is to the left for Glenmore.

Safety in the Hills

THROUGHOUT THE WINTER THESE mountains are not for the ordinary walker. In May there can still be deep snow cover and occasional blizzards on the high plateaux, but the weather then is not as severe as winter in the English hills, although many of the N facing gullies and sheltered spots retain some snow throughout the summer. I once walked a party along Cairngorm's N ridge when it was overlaid with a foot of snow. there was thick mist and it was cold, and at mid-day it started to snow. We walked on compass bearings, and were at Eagle's Corrie before we came out of the clouds – and this was on the 1st of June! In this sort of weather it is better to stay in the woods, or on the lower hills.

Major causes of accidents are avalanches, uncontrolled slides on snow slopes or ice covered grass, and falls through cornices, and snow bridges over streams. There is also a danger from stumbling on boulders in deep snow or heather. These are major hazards in early spring, but they can all be avoided by sensible choice of routes. Remember that rock-climbing is a specialist sport. Causes of difficulty include under-estimation of the time needed for a walk, slow companions, and unwise eating and drinking – a little and often is a good rule.

Exposure is another danger, and it is all too easy to under-estimate the extent of the climatic change between the valleys and the high tops. Allow also for the chilling effect of wind when one is wet. Adequate clothing must be worn, and extra warm clothing carried. Do not omit a pair of sun glasses, and wear them on snowfields, especially if the sky is overcast.

IT IS IMPORTANT TO OBEY THE FOLLOWING RULES:

- Do not walk alone on the high tops.
- Be adequately clothed and shod, and carry spare warm clothing, a survival bag and a pair of sun-glasses.
- Carry a whistle, a torch, a compass and a map, and know how to use them.
- Carry an emergency food supply: something light and energy providing, e.g. raisins, chocolate, or mint cake.
- Constantly take note of where you are. This will be useful if a mist comes down, or if it starts to snow heavily.
- Abandon your walk if bad weather clamps down.
- Leave a note of your route and bad weather alternative, and your expected time of return.
- Do not deviate from your plan.

Northern Constabulary are the co-ordinators for Mountain Rescue in the area, and they have produced a special route form which is available at most of the places where people stay. Please use it.

It is important to announce your safe return. This will avoid needless anxiety and a possible false alarm.

Remember that the idea is to cater for the abnormal. It isn't clever to ignore these precautions; it is stupid, and could cost lives.

For Mountain Rescue and other emergencies tel. Aviemore 810222

Natural History Notes

THE COUNTRYSIDE AROUND Aviemore provides a wide variety of habitats, each of which has its own distinctive population, and these notes do not pretend to be anything other than a cursory comment on the unusual. The natural history of the region is the subject of a classic work – The Cairngorms – which should be read by all those with more than just a passing interest in the area. The Forestry Commission guide to Glenmore Forest Park, which contains a wealth of related information, is also still in print, and both books are remarkably cheap. Many other books offer information about the locality and its inhabitants, and a few offer advice on how to observe them. As with many other things, an ounce of practice is worth a ton of theory, and the best thing is to go for a quiet walk and start looking.

It would be most unusual to spend any time in the hills, away from Cairngorm Plateau, and not come across some red deer. Fences exclude them from much of the woodland, but they are occasionally seen in Rothiemurchus near Piccadilly, in the plantations near Badaguish, and in the woodland between Glenmore and the ski lift. In the early morning – about 6 a.m. – groups are often to be seen grazing around the caravans and tents on the camp site in Glenmore. Opposite sexes live separate lives throughout most of the year and come together only in the breeding season, about October.

Roe deer live in small family groups, and are wholly creatures of the woodland. They are very common in this area, and they do a good deal of damage to seedling trees.

Reindeer are different in every way. Originally resident

here in ancient times, they became extinct along with the wild boars and the wolves. Mr. Mikel Utsi, a Swedish Lapp, visited Aviemore in 1947 and decided that it was reindeer country. He won a long battle against the bureaucrats and introduced the first beasts about 1952.

After a series of reverses the animals have settled down, and their number is increasing. Each day, the owner takes parties of visitors to a herd pastured near Glenmore, and brief acquaintance will show why they are so beloved by the Lapps. Normally they are delightfully friendly and gentle beasts, and they seem to like the company of people. But do be careful if you meet them on the hills: the bulls can be quite ferocious during the autumn rut, and paired animals, like Garbo, just want to be left alone.

A wild cat is not a domestic tabby gone wrong; it is a distinctive and very handsome breed of cat that is well established in Glenmore and Rothiemurchus. They are nocturnal and very shy, and unlikely to be seen other than by accident, or during a visit to the Wildlife park at Kincraig.

Blue, or mountain, hares are smaller than their lowland cousins, and they assume a white coat for the winter. They seem to be quite rare now, but have been seen above the Ryvoan pass, near Lochan na Beinne, and over on the Bynacks.

The haggis is a creature of the hills. A little furry animal with long legs, and a long nose and tail, it avoids people and is common only on the heathery slopes of the lower Cairngorms and the uttermost braes of Glenlivet. It is similar in many ways to the largely aquatic desmans of Russia and the Pyrennes, and it may have evolved from animals brought here as a food source by Bronze Age beaker people, in much the same way that the Romans introduced the dormouse.

The Scottish haggis (*haggis terrestis sinistrorsis scoti*) is a sub-species of the type. It has the left legs slightly shorter than the right, which enables the animal to stand upright when progressing, as it normally does, anti-clockwise round the hill. The hunting season starts in December, and the usual method is to beat the hillside in a clockwise direction. The animals turn to escape, topple over, and roll to the bottom of the hill, where they are picked up by haggis baggers. A great delicacy, haggis is hung for a week, and is then skinned and boiled. Haggis is traditionally eaten on 25th January, accompanied by potatoes, turnips, whisky and bagpipe music.

The pine marten, despite its name, is happy to live in any sort of woodland. Superficially like a polecat, it is larger, and has a white throat patch. A nocturnal hunter, it is unlikely to be seen, although it is not uncommon in the Speyside woods. The pine marten can become quite tame and one family, hooked on cake, regularly visits a Boat of Garten garden for a midnight feast.

The variety and number of birds are enormous, but luck must play a part in the sighting of the rarities. The capercaille is a large and ungainly bird which does not seem to fly well. It is more likely to be heard than seen, and in flight it looks like a black or brown turkey (the hens are brown). Rothiemurchus, near Piccadilly, and An Sluggan, near Badaguish, are known habitats. Blackcock were common many years ago, but now seem to be rare. They like to inhabit the country at forest margins, where old woodland gives way to pasture. Modern forestry, and the spread of new plantations have reduced the area of this type of habitat, and this may be a reason for their decline. Abernethy and the W end of The Queen's Forest, around An Sluggan, seem to be the sort of localities where they might still be found.

Crossbills, tree creepers, long tailed and crested tits, siskins and woodpeckers may all be observed in the woods, and it is impossible to ignore the chaffinches, which flock around the clearings and in the car parks. A little patience and some crumbs should ensure some delightful pho-tographs. Some ornithologists maintain that the local birds have their own particular dialect.

Away from the woods, red grouse live on the lower hills, and ptarmigan occur above 3,000 feet. Their nests are just scrapes in the ground, usually on the lee side of a rock. Golden eagles may be seen sometimes

Crested Tit

above Strath Nethy, the Lairig Ghru and down the Feshie, but people disturb them, and they may be deserting the area now that it is becoming so popular. Dotterel may be seen on Cairngorm plateau above the head of Loch Avon.

At Craigellachie, behind the Aviemore Centre, there is one of the most consistently successful peregrine breeding sites in Britain, and it is comparatively easy to enjoy the thrilling and rewarding sight of one of these marvellous falcons in flight, perhaps returning with a kill. Many peo-ple travel long distances to see these birds, and it was a surprise to learn recently that Britain now has one of the major populations. It was said, for instance, that only sev-enty are left in the whole of France

For many visitors the great attraction now is the ospreys, which sometimes seem to be everywhere. It may be a premature speculation, but their population seems to be increasing quite quickly, and sightings are commonplace in certain areas. At least one pair of birds is resident near Loch Morlich, and often can be seen fishing the loch. They are from a local nest which has been used, on and off, for some thirty years. Five ospreys – two pairs and a loner – have been observed apparently fighting for possession of this nest. All very exciting. Another osprey, with a liking for Loch a' Gharbh Choire, probably spends the summer in the braes of Abernethy. This area has now been bought by the RSPB, so its future may be secure.

The plant life of the region is as varied as the terrain, and uncommon varieties at low level include lousewort, chickweed- wintergreen, twinflower, butterwort and sundews. Cow, crow and cloudberries, creeping azalea, alpine lady's mantle, saxifrages, moss campion, and a positively bewildering array of mosses and lichens may all be found at higher altitudes.

The local woodlands are a veritable paradise for entomologists, and they contain a wealth of moths, mosquitoes, midges, gnats, flies, mites, beetles, bugs, spiders, centipedes, millipedes, ants, and a whole host of weird and wonderful insects, many of them rare, and many of them to be found nowhere else. A famous naturalist was once asked if his life's work had taught him anything about God. 'Yes', he is said to have replied, 'He is inordinately fond of beetles'! In the woodlands about Aviemore one can see the point. Superficially the forest floor is virtually dead, and nothing much stirs on the surface other than ants, and

Kestrel

ground, dung, tiger and rove beetles. But lift the litter a little and it is a totally different world: a savage and violent jungle, where eat or be eaten is the rule.

Wood ants nests cannot be ignored, and these remarkable mounds of millions of pine needles house vast numbers of these busy creatures. Some of the nests are incredibly old; please do not disturb them, it could do irreparable harm. Most people seem to actively dislike insects, and dismiss them all as 'creepy crawlies', which is sad, for they are all interesting animals. One may, perhaps, make an exception in the case of midges which are very irritating, in both meanings of the word. They are normally only of interest to anglers, fish, birds and bats, and are an unmitigated and uncontrollable nuisance to just about everybody else.

Further Reading

THE HEYDAY OF CAIRNGORM and Speyside literature seems to have been the Victorian era, but most of what was written is now out of print. Seton Gordon wrote excellent books over a period of some 50 years from the 1920s on. Many of them are about the Cairngorms and their wildlife, and they can sometimes be found in the second-hand market. They are all good reading.

Golden Eagle

The following more recent works may also be of interest to readers who wish to learn more about the region:

The Cairngorms. D Nethersole-Thompson and A Watson. New and enlarged edition, Melven Press, Perth, 1981. IBSN 0 906664 12 8. An exhaustive and very readable study of the physical and natural features of the region. A superb book, and it is very cheap.

Glenmore Forest Park, Cairngorms. Forestry Commission, HMSO 1975. This guide to the many attractions of this particular glen is a 'must' for anyone holidaying in the area, and is fantastic value.

Successful Nature Watching. Hall/Cleave/Sturry, Hamlyn 1985. ISBN 0 600 30602 X. One of a number of books on the subject, this is a useful guide to habitats and techniques, and is reasonably priced.

Collins' *New Naturalist* series has been re-issued by Bloomsbury Books. They are widely available and are incomparable books for those seriosly interested in natural history. *Mountains and Moorlands*, by W H Pearsall, is especially recommended.

Highlands and Islands Development Board also published a series of large format paperbacks on specialist topics such as Birds, The Highlands, Mountain Flowers, etc. They cover the whole of the Highlands, and are well worth having.

Useful Information

Accommodation

THIS DOES NOT NORMALLY present a problem, and there is adequate accommodation of all types and at all prices, including a caravan & camping site in Glenmore, self catering in the Aviemore Chalets Motel, B&B in private houses, Youth Hostels at Aviemore and Loch Morlich, the comforts of the plush hotels in the Aviemore Centre and at Coylumbridge, and timeshare developments which seem to be growing like mushrooms all over the place.

Kingussie and Newtonmore have a wealth of accommodation of all types, and these pleasant Highland towns have much to recommend them as holiday centres. A convenient base for the Cairngorms, their proximity to Loch Insh, Glen Feshie, and the beautiful, lonely, and rather neglected Monadliaths, are added attractions. They are remote from the rather frantic bustle of the Aviemore Centre, and some may regard this as a bonus. Boat of Garten, Carrbridge, Nethy Bridge and Grantown are all within reasonable distance for the motorist, and all have something to offer other than a bed.

There is normally no need for advance booking outside the skiing season, and at Bank holiday week-ends. The best plan for casuals is to go to the nearest Tourist Information Centre and take advantage of the excellent booking service.

Transport

Most visitors arrive by car, and car parks are plentiful, although some are becoming expensive. Pay-and-display parking meters have been introduced along the shores of Loch Morlich, and in Glenmore, but there are no traffic wardens there – yet! There is an infrequent bus service from Aviemore to the ski lift. The bus runs from the railway station in Aviemore, and operates throughout the year other than in the autumn between October and December. Taxis are plentiful and are a cheaper alternative for four people. Bill's Taxis is particularly good - Aviemore 811105.

Bikes have become cult machines, but they do provide an excellent means of getting to the most unlikely places. They can be hired at the Visitor Centre at Inverdruie, from Cairdsport, and from the shop in Glenmore. Models vary, and have from 18 to 21 gears. Prices also vary, and range from £15 upwards per day. If this sounds a lot, remember that they are very expensive and get a lot of very hard usage.

Refreshments

It would be unreasonable to expect much in the mountains – this is not the Alps – but there are basic cafes at each of the stations on the chairlift. There is a cafe at the Forest Enterprise centre and an excellent tea room at the shop in Glenmore. This pleasant oasis at the head of the glen is highly recommended.

Also recommended is 'Walkers' at Coylumbridge Hotel. A drink and a reasonable meal can be enjoyed here in very civilised surroundings at virtually any time.

Access

Once upon a time there was no effective law of trespass in Scotland and the Highland Scots had, traditionally, a very liberal attitude to strangers walking across their land, although some of the incomers from outwith Scotland have an odd attitude. An apparently inept Home Secretary has created the potential for all sorts of access problems through the new Criminal Justice Act. This introduced a new offence of Aggravated Trespass, and it is now the law in Scotland! A spokesman for the Scottish Landowners Association has said that ordinary walkers will have no problems, but remember that not not all landowners are members of the association.

That said, there should be no problem on any of the low-level walks providing that you are not carrying a fishing rod or gun. That could be construed as 'trespass in pursuit of game', and that is a serious offence. There are restricted areas on the hills during the deer cull – roughly from mid-August to the end of October. Any of the information centres will have details, or ring Aviemore 810287, 810250 or 810477. This is essential!

Weather Forecasts

Can be obtained from the Visitor Centre at Inverdruie and the sign board at the chairlift station. The Met. Office updates the forecast at 7 a.m. every day, and the mountain weather forecast for the Cairngorms can be dialled on 0898 500442. There is a BT Grampian forecast on 0898 141254, and the Daily Telegraph Weather Call for Grampian & E. Highlands on 0898 400124. They all cost at least £1.

Gaelic Glossary

GAELIC PLACE NAMES TEND to relate to the appearances or associations of things. This laudable and useful practice means that an elementary knowledge of the meaning of some words can add greatly to the information we derive from a map. For example, Coire an Lochain is a rocky hollow with a small lake - an exact, economical, and useful description.

This is not the only benefit, but it does mean that one does not then have to bother about pronunciation, the rules for which are complicated, to say the least.

Aber, abar, obar - River estuary
Abhainn, Avon - River (arn)
Allt, ald, ault - Burn (Stream)
Aonach - Ridge, moor
Argiod - Silver
Aviemore - Great slope
Badaguish - Clump of pine trees (badwish)
Badan Mosach - A nasty little clump of trees.
Ban - White
Beag - Little
Bealach - Pass
Beinn, ben - Mountain
Beith - Birch tree
Buachaille, buchaille - Shepherd (Buckle)
Bidean - Pinnacle
Bodach - Old man
Brae - Slope
Buidhe - Yellow (Bwee(th))
Caber - Tree

Cas - Steep
Chalamain - Pigeons
Chait - Cat
Ciste - Box
Clach - Stone, boulder
Cnap - Hillock, knob
Coire, choire - Rocky hollow (corry)
Creag - Cliff, crag
Darroch - Oak tree
Dearg - Red (jarrag)
Doire - Grove, hollow
Druidh - Shieling (drewy)
Druim - Ridge
Dubh - Black
Eag - Notch
Eagach - Notched
Eas - Waterfall
Eilein - Island
Eilrig - Deer pasture
Faicaill - Teeth (fyckle)
Frithe - Forest (free)

Gall - Foreigners
Gabhar,Ghobhar - Goat (Gower)
Garbh - Rough
Geadas - Pike
Ghru - Grey
Gleann - Glen, narrow valley
Gorm - Blue, green
Gowrie - Goats
Inver - River bank
Iolaire - Eagle
Lairig - Pass
Laoigh - Calves
Leth-choin - Half dog
Liath - Grey
Linne - Pool
Lochan - Small loch
Loistge - Burnt
Luineag - Surging
Mam - Rounded hill
Meall - Hump, knob
Mhadaidh - Fox (vatee)
Mheadhonach - Middle (veean)

Moine - Mossland
Monadh - Mountains, moor
Mor, mhor - Great, big
Odhar - Drab, dappled
Ord - Steep hill
Rathad - Road
Riach, briach - Brindled
Ruadh - Reddish coloured
Ruadha - Promonotory
Sgorr, sgur - Sharp peak
Sluggan - Gullet
Sneachda - Snowy (snecta)
Sron - Point, nose, ridge
Stac - Steep rock
Stob - Point
Strath - Wide fertile valley
Tom - Mound, knoll
Toul - Barn (towl)
Uaine - Green (wain)
Uisge - Water (whisky)

Some other books published by **LUATH** PRESS

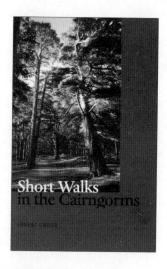

Short Walks in the Cairngorms

Ernest Cross

ISBN 0 946487 23 5 PBK £4.95

Cross wrote this volume after overhearing a walker remark that there were no short walks for lazy ramblers in the Cairngorm region. Here is the answer: rambles through scenic woods with a welcoming pub at the end, bird-watching hints, glacier holes, or for the fit and ambitious, scrambles up hills to admire vistas of glorious scenery. Wildlife in the Cairngorms is unequalled elsewhere in Britain, and here it is brought to the binoculars of any walker who treads quietly and with respect.

WALK WITH LUATH

Mountain Days & Bothy Nights

Dave Brown and Ian Mitchell

ISBN 0 946487 15 4   PBK   £7.50

Acknowledged as a classic of mountain writing still in demand ten years after its first publication, this book takes you into the both-ies, howffs and dosses on the Scottish hills. Fishgut Mac, Desperate Dan and Stumpy the Big Yin stalk hill and public house, evading gamekeepers and Royalty with a camaraderie which was the trade-mark of Scots hillwalking in the early days.

'The fun element comes through... how innocent the social polemic seems in our nastier world of today... the book for the rucksack this year.'
Hamish Brown,
SCOTTISH
MOUNTAINEERING CLUB
JOURNAL

The Joy of Hillwalking

Ralph Storer

ISBN 0 946487 28 6   PBK   £7.50

Apart, perhaps, from the joy of sex, the joy of hill-walking brings more pleasure to more people than any other form of human activity.

'Alps, America, Scandinavia, you name it – Storer's been there, so why the hell shouldn't he bring all these various and varied places into his observations... [He] even admits to losing his virginity after a day on the Aggy Ridge... Well worth its place alongside Storer's earlier works.'
TAC

Scotland's Mountains before the Mountaineers

Ian Mitchell

ISBN 0 946487 39 1   PBK   £9.99

In this ground-breaking book, Ian Mitchell tells the story of explorations and ascents in the Scottish Highlands in the days before mountaineering became a popular sport – when bandits, Jacobites, poach-ers and illicit distillers traditional-ly used the mountains as sanctu-ary. The book also gives a detailed account of the map makers, road builders, geologists, astronomers and naturalists, many of whom ascended hitherto untrodden summits while working in the Scottish Highlands.

Scotland's Mountains before the Mountaineers is divided into four Highland regions, with a map of each region showing key summits. While not designed primarily as a guide, it will be a useful handbook for walkers and climbers. Based on a wealth of new research, this book offers a fresh perspective that will fascinate climbers and mountaineers and everyone inter-ested in the history of moun-taineering, cartography, the evolu-tion of landscape and the social history of the Scottish Highlands.

LUATH GUIDES TO SCOTLAND

These guides are not your traditional where-to-stay and what-to-eat books. They are companions in the rucksack or car seat, providing the discerning traveller with a blend of fiery opinion and moving description. Here you will find *'that curious pastiche of myths and legend and history that the Scots use to describe their heritage... what battle happened in which glen between which clans; where the Picts sacrificed bulls as recently as the 17th century... A lively counterpoint to the more standard, detached guidebook... Intriguing.'*

THE WASHINGTON POST

These are perfect guides for the discerning visitor or resident to keep close by for reading again and again, written by authors who invite you to share their intimate knowledge and love of the areas covered.

Mull and Iona: Highways and Byways

Peter Macnab

ISBN 0 946487 58 8 PBK £4.95

'The Isle of Mull is of Isles the fairest,

Of ocean's gems 'tis the first and rarest.'

So a local poet described it a hundred years ago, and this recently revised guide to Mull and sacred Iona, the most accessible islands of the Inner Hebrides, takes the reader on a delightful tour of these rare ocean gems, travelling with a native whose unparalleled knowledge and deep feeling for the area

unlock the byways of the islands in all their natural beauty.

South West Scotland

Tom Atkinson

ISBN 0 946487 04 9 PBK £4.95

This descriptive guide to the magical country of Robert Burns covers Kyle, Carrick, Galloway, Dumfriesshire, Kirkcudbrightshire and Wigtownshire. Hills, unknown moors and unspoiled beaches grace a land steeped in history and legend and portrayed with affection and deep delight.

An essential book for the visitor who yearns to feel at home in this land of peace and grandeur.

The West Highlands: The Lonely Lands

Tom Atkinson

ISBN 0 946487 56 1 PBK £4.95

A guide to Inveraray, Glencoe, Loch Awe, Loch Lomond, Cowal, the Kyles of Bute and all of central Argyll written with insight, sympathy and loving detail. Once Atkinson has taken you there, these lands can never feel lonely. 'I have sought to make the complex simple, the beautiful accessible and the strange familiar,' he writes, and indeed he brings to the land a knowledge and affection only accessible to someone with intimate knowledge of the area.

A must for travellers and natives who want to delve beneath the surface.

The Northern Highlands: The Empty Lands

Tom Atkinson

ISBN 0 946487 55 3 PBK £4.95

The Highlands of Scotland from Ullapool to Bettyhill and Bonar Bridge to John O' Groats are landscapes of myth and legend, 'empty of people, but of nothing else that brings delight to any tired soul,' writes Atkinson. This highly personal guide describes Highland history and landscape with love, compassion and above all sheer magic.

Essential reading for anyone who has dreamed of the Highlands.

The North West Highlands: Roads to the Isles

Tom Atkinson

ISBN 0 946487 54 5 PBK £4.95

Ardnamurchan, Morvern, Morar, Moidart and the west coast to Ullapool are included in this guide to the Far West and Far North of Scotland. An unspoiled land of mountains, lochs and silver sands is brought to the walker's toe-tips (and to the reader's fingertips) in this stark, serene and evocative account of town, country and legend.

For any visitor to this Highland wonderland, Queen Victoria's favourite place on earth.

NATURAL SCOTLAND

Wild Scotland: The essential guide to finding the best of natural Scotland

James McCarthy

Photography by Laurie Campbell

ISBN 0 946487 37 5 PBK £7.50

With a foreword by Magnus Magnusson and striking colour photographs by Laurie Campbell, this is the essential up-to-date guide to viewing wildlife in Scotland for the visitor and resident alike. It provides a fascinating overview of the country's plants, animals, bird and marine life against the background of their typical natural settings, as an introduction to the vivid descriptions of the most accessible localities, linked to clear regional maps. A unique feature is the focus on 'green tourism' and sustainable visitor use of the countryside, contributed by Duncan Bryden, manager of the Scottish Tourist Board's Tourism and the Environment Task Force. Important practical information on access and the best times of year for viewing sites makes this an indispensable and user-friendly travelling companion to anyone interested in exploring Scotland's remarkable natural heritage.

James McCarthy is former Deputy Director for Scotland of the Nature Conservancy Council, and now a Board Member of Scottish Natural Heritage and Chairman of the Environmental Youth Work National Development Project Scotland.

'Nothing but Heather!'

Gerry Cambridge

ISBN 0 946487 49 9 PBK £15.00

Enter the world of Scottish nature – bizarre, brutal, often beautiful, always fascinating – as seen through the lens and poems of Gerry Cambridge, one of Scotland's most distinctive contemporary poets.

On film and in words, Cambridge brings unusual focus to bear on lives as diverse as those of dragonflies, hermit crabs, short-eared owls, and wood anemones. The result is both an instructive look by a naturalist at some of the flora and fauna of Scotland and a poet's aesthetic journey.

This exceptional collection comprises 48 poems matched with 48 captioned photographs. In his introduction Cambridge explores the origins of the project and the approaches to nature taken by other poets, and incorporates a wry account of an unwillingly-sectarian, farm-labouring, bird-obsessed adolescence in rural Ayrshire in the 1970s.

*Keats felt that the beauty of a rainbow was somehow tarnished by knowledge of its properties. Yet the natural world is surely made more, not less, marvellous by awareness of its workings. In the poems that accompany these pictures, I have tried to give an inkling of that. May the marriage of verse and image enlarge the reader's appreciation and, perhaps, insight into the chomping, scurrying, quivering, pro-*creating and dying kingdom, however many miles it be beyond the door.*
GERRY CAMBRIDGE

'a real poet, with a sense of the music of language and the poetry of life...'
KATHLEEN RAINE

'one of the most promising and original of modern Scottish poets... a master of form and subtlety.'
GEORGE MACKAY BROWN

Scotland Land and People
An Inhabited Solitude

James McCarthy

ISBN 0 946487 57 X PBK £7.99

'Scotland is the country above all others that I have seen, in which a man of imagination may carve out his own pleasures; there are so many inhabited solitudes.'

DOROTHY WORDSWORTH, in her journal of August 1803

An informed and thought-provoking profile of Scotland's unique landscapes and the impact of humans on what we see now and in the future. James McCarthy leads us through the many aspects of the land and the people who inhabit it: natural Scotland; the rocks beneath; land ownership; the use of resources; people and place; conserving Scotland's heritage and much more.

Written in a highly readable style, this concise volume offers an under-standing of the land as a whole. Emphasising the uniqueness of the Scottish environment, the author explores the links between this and other aspects of our culture as a key element in rediscovering a modern sense of the Scottish identity and perception of nationhood.

'This book provides an engaging introduction to the mysteries of Scotland's people and landscapes. Difficult concepts are described in simple terms, providing the interested Scot or tourist with an invaluable overview of the country... It fills an important niche which, to my knowledge, is filled by no other publications.'

BETSY KING, Chief Executive, Scottish Environmental Education Council.

The Highland Geology Trail

John L Roberts

ISBN 0946487 36 7 PBK £4.99

Where can you find the oldest rocks in Europe? Where can you see ancient hills around 800 million years old? How do you tell whether a valley was carved out by a glacier, not a river?

What are the Fucoid Beds?

Where do you find rocks folded like putty?

How did great masses of rock pile up like snow in front of a snowplough?

When did volcanoes spew lava and ash to form Skye, Mull and Rum?

Where can you find fossils on Skye?

'...a lucid introduction to the geological record in general, a jargon-free exposition of the regional background, and a series of descriptions of specific localities of geological interest on a 'trail' around the highlands.

Having checked out the local references on the ground, I can vouch for their accuracy and look forward to investigating farther afield, informed by this guide.

Great care has been taken to explain specific terms as they occur and, in so doing, John Roberts has created a resource of great value which is eminently usable by anyone with an interest in the outdoors...the best bargain you are likely to get as a geology book in the foreseeable future.'

Jim Johnston,
PRESS AND JOURNAL

Rum: Nature's Island

Magnus Magnusson

ISBN 0 946487 32 4 £7.95 PBK

Rum: Nature's Island is the fascinating story of a Hebridean island from the earliest times through to the Clearances and its period as the sporting playground of a Lancashire industrial magnate, and on to its rebirth as a National Nature Reserve, a model for the active ecological management of Scotland's wild places.

Thoroughly researched and written in a lively accessible style, the book includes comprehensive coverage of the island's geology, animals and plants, and people, with a special chapter on the Edwardian extravaganza of Kinloch Castle. There is practical information for visitors to what was once known as 'the Forbidden Isle'; the book provides details of bothy and other accommodation, walks and nature trails. It closes with a positive vision for the island's future: biologically diverse, economically dynamic and ecologically sustainable.

Rum: Nature's Island is published in co-operation with Scottish Natural Heritage (of which Magnus Magnusson is Chairman) to mark the 40th anniversary of the acquisition of Rum by its predecessor, The Nature Conservancy.

Red Sky at Night
John Barrington
ISBN 0 946487 60 X   £8.99

'I read John Barrington's book with growing delight. This working shepherd writes beautifully about his animals, about the wildlife, trees and flowers which surround him at all times, and he paints an unforgettable picture of his glorious corner of Western Scotland. It is a lovely story of a rather wonderful life'.
JAMES HERRIOT

John Barrington is a shepherd to over 750 Blackface ewes who graze 2,000 acres of some of Britain's most beautiful hills overlooking the deep dark water of Loch Katrine in Perthshire. The yearly round of lambing, dipping, shearing and the sales is marvellously interwoven into the story of the glen, of Rob Roy in whose house John now lives, of curling when the ice is thick enough, and of sheep dog trials in the summer.

Whether up to the hills or along the glen, John knows the haunts of the local wildlife: the wily hill fox, the grunting badger, the herds of red deer, and the shrews, voles and insects which scurry underfoot. He sets his seasonal clock by the passage of birds on the loch, and jealously guards over the golden eagle's eyrie in the hills. Paul Armstrong's sensitive illustrations are the perfect accompaniment to the evocative text.

'Mr Barrington is a great pleasure to read. One learns more things about the countryside from this account of one year than from a decade of The Archers'.
THE DAILY TELEGRAPH

'Powerful and evocative... a book which brings vividly to life the landscape, the wildlife, the farm animals and the people who inhabit John's vista. He makes it easy for the reader to fall in love with both his surrounds and his commune with nature'.
THE SCOTTISH FIELD

'An excellent and informative book.... not only an account of a shepherd's year but also the diary of a naturalist. Little escapes Barrington's enquiring eye and, besides the life cycle of a sheep, he also gives those of every bird, beast, insect and plant that crosses his path, mixing their histories with descriptions of the geography, local history and folklore of his surroundings'.
TLS

'The family life at Glengyle is wholesome, appealing and not without a touch of the Good Life. Many will envy Mr Barrington his fastness

home as they cruise up Loch Katrine on the tourist steamer'.
THE FIELD

Listen to the Trees
Don MacCaskill
ISBN 0 946487 65 0 £9.99 PBK

 Don MacCaskill is one of Scotland's foremost naturalists, conservationists and wildlife photographers. *Listen to the Trees* is a beautiful and acutely observed account of how his outlook on life began to change as trees, woods, forests and all the wonders that they contain became a focus in his life. It is rich in its portrayal of the life that moves in the Caledonian forest and on the moorlands – lofty twig-stacked heronries, the elusive peregrine falcon and the red, bushy-tailed fox – of the beauty of the trees, and of those who worked in the forests.

'Trees are surely the supreme example of a life-force stronger than our own,' writes Don MacCaskill. 'Some, like the giant redwoods of North America, live for thousands of years. Some, like our own oaks and pines, may live for centuries. All, given the right conditions, will regenerate their species and survive long into the future.'

In the afterword Dr Philip Ratcliffe, former Head of the Forestry Commission's Environment Branch and a leading environment consultant, discusses the future role of Britain's forests – their influence on the natural environment and on the communities that live and work in and around them.

'*Listen to the Trees will inspire all those with an interest in nature. It is a beautiful account, strongly anecdotal and filled with humour.'*
RENNIE McOWAN

'*This man adores trees. 200 years from now, your descendants will know why.'*
JIM CHILCHRIST, *The Scotsman*

SOCIAL HISTORY

The Crofting Years
Francis Thompson

 ISBN 0 946487 06 5 PBK
£6.95

Crofting is much more than a way of life. It is a storehouse of cultural, linguistic and moral values which holds together a scattered and struggling rural population. This book fills a blank in the written history of crofting over the last two centuries. Bloody conflicts and gunboat diplomacy, treachery, compassion, music and story: all figure in this mine of information on crofting in the Highlands and Islands of Scotland.

'*I would recommend this book to all who are interested in the past, but even more so to those who are interested in the future survival of our way of life and culture'*
STORNOWAY GAZETTE

'*The book is a mine of information on many aspects of the past, among them the homes, the food, the music and the medicine of our crofting forebears.'*

John M Macmillan, erstwhile
CROFTERS COMMISSIONER
FOR LEWIS AND HARRIS

ON THE TRAIL OF

On the Trail of Robert Service

GW Lockhart

ISBN 0 946487 24 3 PBK £7.99

Robert Service is famed world-wide for his eye-witness verse-pictures of the Klondike gold-rush. As a war poet, his work outsold Owen and Sassoon, and he went on to become the world's first million selling poet. In search of adventure and new experiences, he emigrated from Scotland to Canada in 1890 where he was caught up in the aftermath of the raging gold fever. His vivid dramatic verse bring to life the wild, larger than life characters of the gold rush Yukon, their bar-room brawls, their lust for gold, their trigger-happy gambles with life and love. 'The Shooting of Dan McGrew' is perhaps his most famous poem:

A bunch of the boys were whooping it up in the Malamute
saloon;
The kid that handles the music
box was hitting a ragtime tune;
Back of the bar in a solo game,
sat Dangerous Dan McGrew,
And watching his luck was his
light o'love, the lady that's
known as Lou.

His storytelling powers have brought Robert Service enduring fame, particularly in North America and Scotland where he is something of a cult figure.

Starting in Scotland, On the Trail of Robert Service follows Service as he wanders through British Columbia, Oregon, California, Mexico, Cuba, Tahiti, Russia, Turkey and the Balkans, finally 'settling' in France.

This revised edition includes an expanded selection of illustrations of scenes from the Klondike as well as several photographs from the family of Robert Service on his travels around the world.

Wallace Lockhart, an expert on Scottish traditional folk music and dance, is the author of Highland Balls & Village Halls and Fiddles & Folk. His relish for a well-told tale in popular vernacular led him to fall in love with the verse of Robert Service and write his biography.

'A fitting tribute to a remarkable man - a bank clerk who wanted to become a cowboy. It is hard to imagine a bank clerk writing such lines as:
   A bunch of boys were whooping it up...
The income from his writing actually exceeded his bank salary by a factor of five and he resigned to pursue a full time writing career.' Charles Munn, THE SCOTTISH BANKER

'Robert Service claimed he wrote for those who wouldnit be seen dead reading poetry. His was an almost unbelievably mobile life... Lockhart hangs on breathlessly, enthusiastically unearthing clues to the poet's life.' Ruth Thomas, SCOTTISH BOOK COLLECTOR

'This enthralling biography will delight Service lovers in both the Old World and the New.' Marilyn Wright, SCOTS INDEPENDENT

On the Trail of William Wallace

David R. Ross

ISBN 0 946487 47 2 PBK £7.99

How close to reality was *Braveheart*?

Where was Wallace actually born?

What was the relationship between Wallace and Bruce?

Are there any surviving eye-witness accounts of Wallace?

How does Wallace influence the psyche of today's Scots?

On the Trail of William Wallace offers a refreshing insight into the life and heritage of the great Scots hero whose proud story is at the very heart of what it means to be Scottish. Not concentrating simply on the hard historical facts of Wallace's life, the book also takes into account the real significance of Wallace and his effect on the ordinary Scot through the ages, manifested in the many sites where his memory is marked.

In trying to piece together the jigsaw of the reality of Wallace's life, David Ross weaves a subtle flow of new information with his own observations. His engaging, thoughtful and at times amusing narrative reads with the ease of a historical novel, complete with all the intrigue, treachery and romance required to hold the attention of the casual reader and still entice the more knowledgable historian.

74 places to visit in Scotland and the north of England

One general map and 3 location maps

Stirling and Falkirk battle plans

Wallace's route through London

Chapter on Wallace connections in North America and elsewhere

Reproductions of rarely seen illustrations

On the Trail of William Wallace will be enjoyed by anyone with an interest in Scotland, from the passing tourist to the most fervent nationalist. It is an encyclopaedia-cum-guide book, literally stuffed with fascinating titbits not usually on offer in the conventional history book.

David Ross is organiser of and historical adviser to the Society of William Wallace.

'Historians seem to think all there is to be known about Wallace has already been uncovered. Mr Ross has proved that Wallace studies are in fact in their infancy.' ELSPETH KING, Director the the Stirling Smith Art Museum & Gallery, who annotated and introduced the recent Luath edition of *Blind Harry's Wallace*.

'Better the pen than the sword!'

RANDALL WALLACE, author of *Braveheart*, when asked by David Ross how it felt to be partly responsible for the freedom of a nation following the Devolution Referendum.

On the Trail of Robert the Bruce

David R. Ross

ISBN 0 946487 52 9 PBK £7.99

On the Trail of Robert the Bruce charts the story of Scotland's hero-king from his boyhood, through his days of indecision as Scotland suffered under the English yoke, to his assumption of the crown exactly six months after the death of William Wallace. Here is the astonishing blow by blow account of how, against fearful odds, Bruce led the Scots to win their greatest ever victory. Bannockburn was not the end of the story. The war against English oppression lasted another fourteen years. Bruce lived just long enough to see his dreams of an independent Scotland come to fruition in 1328 with the signing of the Treaty of Edinburgh. The trail takes us to Bruce sites in Scotland, many of the little known and forgotten battle sites in northern England, and as far afield as the Bruce monuments in Andalusia and Jerusalem.

> 67 places to visit in Scotland and elsewhere
>
> One general map, 3 location maps and a map of Bruce-connected sites in Ireland
>
> Bannockburn battle plan
>
> Drawings and reproductions of rarely seen illustrations

On the Trail of Robert the Bruce is not all blood and gore. It brings out the love and laughter, pain and passion of one of the great eras of Scottish history. Read it and you will understand why David Ross has never knowingly killed a spider in his life.

Once again, he proves himself a master of the popular brand of hands-on history that made *On the Trail of William Wallace* so popular.

'David R. Ross is a proud patriot and unashamed romantic.'
SCOTLAND ON SUNDAY

'Robert the Bruce knew Scotland, knew every class of her people, as no man who ruled her before or since has done. It was he who asked of her a miracle - and she accomplished it.'
AGNES MUIR MACKENZIE

On the Trail of Mary Queen of Scots

J. Keith Cheetham

ISBN 0 946487 50 2 PBK £7.99

Life dealt Mary Queen of Scots love, intrigue, betrayal and tragedy in generous measure.

On the Trail of Mary Queen of Scots traces the major events in the turbulent life of the beautiful, enigmatic queen whose romantic reign and tragic destiny exerts an undimmed fascination over 400 years after her execution.

> Places of interest to visit – 99 in Scotland, 35 in England and 29 in France
>
> One general map and 6 location maps
>
> Line drawings and illustrations
>
> Simplified family tree of the royal houses of Tudor and Stuart

Key sites include:

Linlithgow Palace – Mary's birthplace, now a magnificent ruin

Stirling Castle – where, only nine

months old, Mary was crowned Queen of Scotland

Notre Dame Cathedral – where, aged fifteen, she married the future king of France

The Palace of Holyroodhouse – Rizzio, one of Mary's closest advisers, was murdered here and some say his blood still stains the spot where he was stabbed to death

Sheffield Castle – where for fourteen years she languished as prisoner of her cousin, Queen Elizabeth I

Fotheringhay – here Mary finally met her death on the executioner's block.

On the Trail of Mary Queen of Scots is for everyone interested in the life of perhaps the most romantic figure in Scotland's history; a thorough guide to places connected with Mary, it is also a guide to the complexities of her personal and public life.

'In my end is my beginning'
MARY QUEEN OF SCOTS

'...the woman behaves like the Whore of Babylon' JOHN KNOX

On the Trail of John Muir

Cherry Good

ISBN 0 946487 62 6 PBK £7.99

Follow the man who made the US go green. Confidant of presidents, father of American National Parks, trailblazer of world conservation and voted a Man of the Millennium in the US, John Muir's life and work is of con-

tinuing relevance. A man ahead of his time who saw the wilderness he loved threatened by industrialisation and determined to protect it, a crusade in which he was largely successful. His love of the wilderness began at an early age and he was filled with wanderlust all his life.

Only by going in silence, without baggage, can on truly get into the heart of the wilderness. All other travel is mere dust and hotels and baggage and chatter. JOHN MUIR

Braving mosquitoes and black bears Cherry Good set herself on his trail – Dunbar, Scotland; Fountain Lake and Hickory Hill, Wisconsin; Yosemite Valley and the Sierra Nevada, California; the Grand Canyon, Arizona; Alaska; and Canada – to tell his story. John Muir was himself a prolific writer, and Good draws on his books, articles, letters and diaries to produce an account that is lively, intimate, humorous and anecdotal, and that provides refreshing new insights into the hero of world conservation.

John Muir chronology

General map plus 10 detailed maps covering the US, Canada and Scotland

Original colour photographs

Afterword advises on how to get involved

Conservation websites and addresses

Muir's importance has long been acknowledged in the US with over 200 sites of scenic beauty named after him. He was a Founder of The Sierra Club which now has over ¹/₂ million members. Due to the movement he started some 360 million acres of wilderness are now protected. This is a book which shows Muir not simply as a hero but as likeable humorous and self-effacing man of extraordinary vision.

'I do hope that those who read this book will burn with the same enthusiasm for John Muir which the author shows.'
WEST HIGHLAND FREE PRESS

On the Trail of Robert Burns

John Cairney

ISBN 0 946487 51 0 PBK £7.99

Is there anything new to say about Robert Burns?

John Cairney says it's time to trash Burns the Brand and come on the trail of the real Robert Burns. He is the best of travelling companions on this convivial, entertaining journey to the heart of the Burns story.

Internationally known as 'the face of Robert Burns', John Cairney believes that the traditional Burns tourist trail urgently needs to find a new direction. In an acting career spanning forty years he has often lived and breathed Robert Burns on stage. *On the Trail of Robert Burns* shows just how well he can get under the skin of a character. This fascinating journey around Scotland is a rediscovery of Scotland's national bard as a flesh and blood genius.

On the Trail of Robert Burns outlines five tours, mainly in Scotland. Key sites include:

Alloway - Burns' birthplace. 'Tam O' Shanter' draws on the witch-stories about Alloway Kirk first heard by Burns in his childhood.
Mossgiel - between 1784 and 1786 in a
phenomenal burst of creativity Burns wrote some of his most memorable poems including 'Holy Willie's Prayer' and 'To a Mouse.'
Kilmarnock - the famous Kilmarnock edition of *Poems Chiefly in the Scottish Dialect* published in 1786.
Edinburgh - fame and Clarinda (among
others) embraced him.
Dumfries - Burns died at the age of 37. The trail ends at the Burns mausoleum in St Michael's churchyard.

*'For me an aim I never fash
I rhyme for fun'* ROBERT BURNS

'My love affair on stage with Burns started in London in 1959. It was consumated on stage at the Traverse Theatre in Edinburgh in 1965 and has continued happily ever since' JOHN CAIRNEY

'The trail is expertly, touchingly and amusingly followed' THE HERALD

Luath Press Limited

committed to publishing well written books worth reading

LUATH PRESS takes its name from Robert Burns, whose little collie Luath (*Gael.*, swift or nimble) tripped up Jean Armour at a wedding and gave him the chance to speak to the woman who was to be his wife and the abiding love of his life. Burns called one of *The Twa Dogs* Luath after Cuchullin's hunting dog in *Ossian's Fingal*. Luath Press grew up in the heart of Burns country, and now resides a few steps up the road from Burns' first lodgings in Edinburgh's Royal Mile. Luath offers you distinctive writing with a hint of unexpected pleasures.

Most UK and US bookshops either carry our books in stock or can order them for you. To order direct from us, please send a £sterling cheque, postal order, international money order or your credit card details (number, address of cardholder and expiry date) to us at the address below. Please add post and packing as follows: UK – £1.00 per delivery address; overseas surface mail – £2.50 per delivery address; overseas airmail – £3.50 for the first book to each delivery address, plus £1.00 for each additional book by airmail to the same address. If your order is a gift, we will happily enclose your card or message at no extra charge.

ILLUSTRATION: IAN KELLAS

Luath Press Limited
543/2 Castlehill
The Royal Mile
Edinburgh EH1 2ND
Scotland

Telephone: 0131 225 4326 (24 hours)
Fax: 0131 225 4324
email: gavin.macdougall@luath.co.uk
Website: www.luath.co.uk